THESE CROOKED FINGERS

Copyright © 2020 Makepeace Deorji
All rights reserved. First paperback edition printed 2019 in the
United Kingdom
a catalogue record for this book is available
from the British Library.
ISBN 978-1-913455-12-5
No part of this book shall be reproduced or transmitted in any
form or by
any means, electronic or mechanical, including photocopying,
recording, or by any information retrieval system without
written permission of the publisher.
Published by Scribblecity Publications.
Printed in Great Britain
Although every precaution has been taken in
the preparation of this book, the publisher and author assume
no responsibility for errors or omissions. Neither is any liability
assumed for damages resulting from the use of this information
contained herein.

This work is dedicated particularly to my mum, Mrs. Eucharia Deorji nee Okorafor who for her love for education and passion to see her children educated tried her hands at various ventures in order to secure her children's education and to all women all over the world who work with their hands to make their families, places of work and the society at large a better place.

GRATITUDE

To God Almighty:

My Inspirer,

My Mentor,

My Muse!

CHARACTERS

FANCY	Flair's best friend
FLAIR	Fancy's best friend
MAMA OLUAKA	Seller of fried foods
OLUCHI	Mama Oluaka's only daughter
1ST MAN	Buyer of fries
2ND MAN	Buyer of fries
LITTLE GIRL	Buyer of fries
YOUNG WOMAN	Buyer of fries
MADAM HUSTLE	Seller of fresh vegetables
MADAM ACTION	Trader in beans and other grains
OBIKE	1ST YOUTH
SILAS	2ND YOUTH
CLETUS	3RD YOUTH
LINUS	MALE TRADER
ABILITY	Son to Linus
DAME	Beautician
DR. BENT	Son to Mrs. Oluaka
ENGR. REWARD	Son to Mrs. Oluaka

TABLE OF CONTENTS

Prologue	7
Scene 1	14
Scene 2	23
Scene 3	37
Scene 4	60
Scene 5	65
Scene 6	80
Scene 7	88
Epilogue	113
Glossary	115

PROLOGUE

(A clownish person appears on stage wearing a worn out shirt and trousers with tattered, mismatching shoes. At the back of his old, brown-like, threadbare shirt is a boldly written inscription "SLUGGARD".)

SLUGGARD *(He paces about the stage aimlessly; dangling from side to side, lying down, getting up, and looking about furtively while bemoaning his fate)* I have searched; I have searched; I have paced about these streets in search of a job, a well paying job and have found none these five years. *(Stops abruptly)* Yes, I do remember that before the past five years that I have done some form of work as a teacher but, I don't want just any job. I am a graduate for heaven's sake, a sound one at that. I made a 2:1 and therefore deserve something better. I deserve something better than what they were offering and so I quit and have since then been searching. *(Thinking)* Why should I take to such jobs that hardly

Prologue

meet my needs, jobs that pay me pennies? (*Conclusively*) No way!

(*Entering the stage is another clown, she is dressed in a long flowing blue gown with the inscription "WORK" written all over it.*)

WORK   (*Appealing to Sluggard*) Come, take me!
SLUGGARD   (*Complainingly*) No, I am tired. I have no strength in me to take you, no.
WORK   (*Looks about her assertively*) Why not? Why won't you have me? I am profitable. I have reward with me?
SLUGGARD   (*Looks WORK up and down as though assessing her worth*) Reward, did you say reward? What's your reward worth?
WORK   (*Reminiscing*) I guess how much you put into me determines how much you get as a reward.
SLUGGARD   (*Laughs mirthlessly*) Guess, you are guessing? No! Your reward is discriminatory, if I put in eight hours into you as a teacher what's my reward's worth? And if I were to put in the same number of hours into you as a medical doctor, what would my reward be? Are they same?
(*WORK is silent.*)
SLUGGARD   (*Irritated*) Answer me?
WORK   (*Yet reminiscing*) You see, before you put in

eight hours into me as a medical doctor; you must have spent at least seven trying to get yourself equipped. You input so much money in paying fees, buying books, gadgets and the eight hours you spend is spent trying to save lives. While, should you decide to put in eight hours into me as a teacher and consider my reward too small; you will have to bear in mind that you only put in four years to equip yourself with far less money for fees and buying of books. Although your job requires that you mould lives for the best; they'd have to be alive first for you to have to do that.

SLUGGARD *(Under his breath, pointing angrily at WORK)* Your unequal reward is your undoing. Why should I choose you with your unequal scale, measuring and weighing balances? *(Pacing about restively)* Don't you worry, your reward is negligible (*Continues to pace about, thinking, his right hand to his head scratching)* one of our neighbours is a highly placed man in the army; I think I should meet him. Perhaps, he will find me something to do; something that fetches real money. Perhaps, he'd recruit me into the army where I hear they earn so much from peace keeping to

Prologue

WORK
being sent to crisis prone zones for security purposes within the country. *(Appealing)* Well, how about you do something with your *(Pointing at Sluggard's hands)* hands, say plumbing, carpentry? Say you start an enterprise of your own, get your own money, employ people and get them to work for you? *(Gleefully joins her hands together and lifts them to her chin)* Wouldn't that be wonderful?

SLUGGARD
(Quiet for a while and then almost abruptly, he paces about the stage confidently) Perhaps I should join the yahoo, yahoo boys or internet gurus and make some cool dough; story has it that they make lots of money. *(As though coming upon a certain idea)* Ah! Ha! How about I take to gambling, or the betting games? The money comes real quickly.

(WORK brings her hands down and looks at him disdainfully.)

(Playfully touches her chin): Come on, betting is legal. I mean who doesn't indulge in it from time to time these days? Think of it, with just fifty naira, I could win millions of naira. All I need do is learn the nitty-gritty of the game *(Jumps*

	up in glee.) With that kind of win, what need would I have *(Scornfully raises his and at WORK)* of you?
WORK	*(Convincingly)* Wealth gotten by vanity shall reduce! But if you gather by labour, you will increase.
SLUGGARD	*(Gives WORK a mocking look)* Increase indeed, by labour? Work is hard! So, tell me, who are those increasing? The farmers who hardly have subsidies, who hardly have access to fertilizers, who still use local tools and yet produce little or nothing for sale? Oh! Or are you referring to teachers, those of them who teach in private nursery, primary and secondary schools, whose reward is in heaven? *(Laughs disapprovingly)* Leave me alone; I have no need of you. Why can't I stay at home, do something on my computer and earn some cool mint. I mean it's work too, isn't it?
WORK	*(Walking close to him, holding him by his right arm)* Come, come, is it me you are talking about or are you talking about duping people, stealing from people or engaging in internet fraud? Why not take me instead? I am honest, straightforward. The sleep of a labouring

Prologue

	man is sweet.
SLUGGARD	*(Quietly withdrawing his arm from WORK's hold)* No. I refuse to labour. Labour! Labour! Labour! *(Miserable)* Whatever happened to favour, good luck?
WORK	*(Heaves a sigh of disappointment)* These will come while you are busy with me. He that labours labours for himself, for his mouth craves it of him. If you do not have me, you ought not to eat, you know?
SLUGGARD	*(smiling slowly, hands akimbo)* Tell me; what portion of you is in use when people sit about their offices in the helms of the affairs of this nation daily doing nothing only to be paid fat salaries at the end of the month?
WORK	*(Crestfallen)* That's not a part of me at all. It's an abuse of me? When people get rewarded without me; it's corruption!
SLUGGARD	*(Confused)* Abuse, corruption?
WORK	*(Nodding her head in acknowledgment)* Yes!
	(SLUGGARD is silent.)
WORK	*(Anxious, taking him by the hands)* So, will you take me now?
SLUGGARD	*(Looks at her as though trying to weigh his options and then he shakes his head negatively)* No, I won't. I have no strength

	for you.
WORK	*(Falls to SLUGGARD's feet holding lightly to them)* The desire of the slothful kills him for his hands refuse to labour. Look at the ants; they are a people not strong yet they prepare their meat in the summer.
SLUGGARD	*(Wriggles his feet free from WORK's hold and walks away)* I am no ant!
WORK	*(Getting up gradually)* Go to the ants, you sluggard, consider her ways and be wise!

(Runs after SLUGGARD as Curtain falls!)

END OF PROLOGUE

SCENE 1

(10:45pm, Friday night. In Ms. Flair's bedroom. Fancy, Flair's best friend is seated on a bed watching a late night fashion show on television. She is fair skinned; the fairness that comes from using too much complexion creams and soaps. Her hair is covered in a black and yellow coloured hair net and she has on a silky-white nightgown. With her eyes glued to the television, she chews away at popcorns from a popcorn cup held tightly in her left hand as her right hand guides the popcorns into her mouth. She intermittently looks at an engagement ring firmly placed in the middle finger of her left hand as she chews.)

FANCY (*Chewing roughly as she wriggles her small body*): This gown does make a lot of sense. Oh! How I wish I could wear this during my wedding reception. *(Wriggles yet again)* Wait, how many times did the Duchess of Sussex have to change her clothing on her wedding day?
(Flair enters her bedroom looking exhausted with a beaded black bag in her left hand. She is dark in complexion and has on a light green

	A-line gown.)
FLAIR	*(A surprised look on her face as she sees Fancy still awake watching the television):* Are you kidding me?
FANCY	*(Not turning to look at her, still chewing)* Kidding you, how?
FLAIR	*(Disappointingly drops the beaded bag on the bed; walks towards the television, switches it off turns and faces Fancy staring hard at her, hands akimbo, head shaking questioningly)* What do you think you're doing staying up late this night just to watch a fashion show girlfriend?
FANCY	*(Carelessly drops the popcorn cup on the floor after taking the last contents of the cup and putting them in her mouth.)* What is it this time Flair? What would you have me do? what?
FLAIR	*(Still starring hard at her)* You know, if only you watch these fashion shows so you can learn how to sew a piece or two; I wouldn't really mind; it wouldn't really bother me.
FANCY	*(Raising both hands questioningly)* Really? I can't get to sew any one of them clothes and how's that a problem Flair?
FLAIR	*(Heaves a deep sigh as she begins to make gestures with her hands)* You know I have been hoping you'd at least find something

Scene 1

FANCY	doing with your hands; say, try a skill. *(Eyelids flickering in disbelief)* What? Can you just listen to yourself Flair? You are asking me, Fancy to learn a skill after obtaining a Master's Degree in Economics from the Coast University in Walium? You aren't serious I suppose. Look at my hands, my fingers *(She stretches them out and looks at them carefully)* as supple and soft as they are, you want me to toughen them, over what, beads and motif like you just to make a beaded bag of how much?

FLAIR	*(Calmly, walking towards the bed to Fancy.)* Look, I know the income at first may not be grand but then it's a start. As they say, half a loaf is better than nothing.

FANCY	*(Frustrated)* Are you lecturing me now? I don't get this. Are you my mother now? *(Disinterested)* Please cut me some slack will you? I am staying over at your place these few days because your house is close to my fiancé's; that doesn't give you the right to lecture me, okay. I already had enough of lectures at the university alright? *(Her right hand to her forehead.)*

FLAIR	*(Sitting quietly beside Fancy on the bed)* Listen Fancy *(Takes both her hands in hers)* I am sorry I sounded harsh; but dear, you know the state of the nation and the economy now; there are no jobs and because there are no jobs; we are expected to create them. I am a graduate too. Granted, I don't have a master's degree yet but then I did job hunt for five years and found none. After the sixth year I had to tell myself the truth that I can do something about my unemployed state. Not everyone will have the opportunity to get at jobs; some will have to create them. I hope to be a job creator and am working at it. I cannot be an employer of labour without first finding something doing myself from whence I hope to employ others.

FANCY *(Eyes welling up with tears)* I am not cut out to work with my hands Flair. Don't you understand? I don't have passion for handwork be it sewing, cooking, writing, crafting, moulding, just any of those things. Not everyone is cut out for menial work; I mean that's why I got educated in the first place, so I don't get to do menial work; isn't it?

FLAIR *(Speaking in a low reassuring tone while tapping mildly at Fancy's fingers)* Yes. Not everyone is cut out to work with their hands, Fancy. But life happens to us all! I believe

Scene 1

	it's wisdom for one to work with one's hands, especially when there's nothing else to do. We need to work to eat Fancy, to get at all the good things we desire in life. And we can't keep waiting for a job to come by before we do something. I mean how long are you going to have to depend on your parents? Have you thought about that? It's a great thing you have your master's degree; all you need do is sit down and think what best you are good at and then give it a shot. *(Smiling)* Your master's degree gives you leverage over others who do not have one you know?
FANCY	*(Smiling more to herself, she takes a glance at her engagement ring)* Well, it's a good thing I will be getting married pretty soon and when this happens; I will certainly not be a burden to my parents no more.
FLAIR	*(Giving her a concerned look)* And you are sure your fiancé wouldn't mind? I mean, how many men these days take delight in marrying non-financial women? Life is hard you know; so these days we have husbands bringing in something into the home as well as wives to make the home stable. But when it's just one person paying the bills, *(Shrugs her shoulders in exasperation)* I think that can cause friction in the home.

FANCY	*(Quietly withdrawing her fingers from Flair's hold as she cuddles herself up in thought)* Well, some men may not afford to marry non-financial women, but not my beloved Bent *(Smiles as she gives Flair a knowing look.)* He's not like the regular guys. He's that kind of man who believes that a man should fend for his family and not necessarily depend on his wife for assistance to ensure the family's survival. He doesn't mind that I am not working. He's very caring, loving, understanding and supportive. He knows I am not incapacitated because I am educated.
FLAIR	*(Heaves a sigh of relief)* Good gracious! I am relieved to hear this.
FANCY	*(Refrains from cuddling herself and takes Flair's hands tenderly)* Don't be overly worried about me *(makes a funny face)* mother! I can very well take care of myself, mnnh.
FLAIR	*(Looks at her concernedly)* Fan, you are sure you will be okay. I mean there's no harm in starting a business you love, you can always ask your fiancé for capital to start up.
FANCY	*(whirls her head around)* Oh! My girlfriend, can we just stop this already? You're killing me.
FLAIR	*(submitting)* Fanny, I care. I know of a few homes where wives are caged, made

Scene 1

	incompetent and relegated to the background simply because they have nothing doing but solely depend on their husbands for money. You wouldn't want that for yourself would you?
FANCY	*(becoming serious faced)* No I wouldn't. I will get a job, okay
FLAIR	*(Nodding)* Okay
FANCY	*(Smiling once again)* You worry too much mother.
FLAIR	I care Fancy.
FANCY	*(Giving her a mock angry look)* Yes, way too much you care. If you care, you wouldn't let me sweep around your house these past three days or wash the dishes or mop your kitchen floor.
FLAIR	*(Folding her hands and feigning serious)* Oh! Yeah! So, you want to make it obvious to my parents that you are a lazy been-to who wouldn't do the slightest work, right? Well, not under my watch. What do you think they'd say to me when you're gone, that I have a lazy bag for a friend?
FANCY	*(Shrugs her shoulders)* Your parents are damn authoritative. How do you thrive under them?
FLAIR	*(Smiles ruefully)* I am doing very well aye; you can see that for yourself can't you?

FANCY	*(Nodding idly)* Yeah, I very well can see that. *(Looks at the alarm clock placed at Flair's beside table)* Oh! My!
FLAIR	*(Agitated):* What is it?
FANCY	It's 12am!
FLAIR	*(wide eyed)* Are you serious? *(Looking towards her beside mirror to the clock)* I have to catch some sleep *(To Fancy)* See what you've caused?
FANCY	*(Surprised)* Me, how?
	(Flair quickly gets off the bed, takes the beaded bag and keeps it on her reading table; she heads back to the bed and begins to find her way under the covers of her duvet.)
	Wait, are you going to bed, not having your night gown on? *(Turning her head in disbelief)* I don't remember seeing you run a bath for the night.
FLAIR	*(Turning away from her)* I don't have the time for that Flair. I need to catch some sleep. It will soon be daylight and you know I'll have to prepare breakfast for my parents before they head to work by six to beat the traffic.
FANCY	*(Remembering)* Yes, that reminds me. You promised you would take me to the bean ball seller who sold to you the fried sweet potatoes, plantain, yam and bean balls we

Scene 1

	ate for breakfast day before yesterday I really love her bean balls; they are so well made. Where I live at Kwata Estate; the women who sell bean balls there mix their bean flour with maize flour just to make excess gain. *(With zeal)* So, you'll take me to the bean ball seller right? Flair, *(No response)*. Flair!
FLAIR	*(Mumbles)* Yes. Just go to bed. We won't be able to buy from the seller if you happen to wake at your usual 8 o'clock. She sells between 5am to 7am. You were still asleep when I returned from my purchase day before yesterday, remember?
FANCY	*(Giving in)* Alright mother! *(She begins to find her way under the duvet as Light fades)*

END OF SCENE 1

SCENE 2

(The wee hours of the morning with a nightly, not too clear weather Under a shade by the road side is a slim, middle aged woman, fair in complexion in near faded wrapper, blouse and head gear; she is busy turning with a long frying spoon the contents of a large frying pan which is well balanced on a three thronged tripod stand with firewood emitting fire under the frying pan to help fry its contents. She has about her waist a dark blue coloured apron, her bank, wherein she puts her monies from the day's sales. She is MAMA OLUAKA popularly called "Mama Akara" for her frying bean balls alongside other "fries". With her is her daughter, OLUCHI who is busy helping her mother with adding firewood to the few sticks of firewood under the frying pan and blowing at them so as to get at more fire from them.

Under the make shift shelter which belonged to MAMA OLUAKA, a few wooden tables and benches are arranged to make provision for customers who would want to eat there. An extended high table is also visible; on this table are four transparent plastic bowls with lids. The first transparent plastic bowl is labelled "Fried Akara", while the second to the fourth

scene 2

plastics are labelled "Fried Yam", "Fried Sweet Potato" and "Fried Plantain" respectively. Also on this table are packets of black polythene bags and a deep bowl inside which are three forks of different sizes and shapes. In between the four bowls is a medium sized pot with sauce made from pepper, tomatoes and onions fried in palm oil.)

MAMA OLUAKA (*In a loud tone*): Akara! Akara! Akara *di oku!* Come for your tasty, hot akara; your delicious sweet potato, yam and plantain. I fried them well; they are sizeable and tasty and yet for only five Naira. Come my dear customers, come. Mama Akara is here again. I will give you jara.

1ST MAN Mama Akara good morning. Give me akara fifty naira, potatoes thirty naira, and yam seventy Naira; please be fast.

MMA OLUAKA (*Smiling cheerfully*) Good morning Sir; I am at your service. (*Takes up a black polythene bag, opens it and with a fork she begins to put into it the items demanded by the customer*).

MAMA OLUAKA Do you want me to add sauce to it?

1ST MAN Yes. How do I eat the sweet potatoes and yam without sauce? Please put enough.

MAMA OLUAKA Alright (*Begins to add the sauce from the sauce pot*)
(*A second man approaches Mama Oluaka's shade*)

2ND MAN	Mama Akara, give me akara hundred naira, yam hundred naira, and plantain fifty naira. Please hurry up; I am hurrying off to work; I need to beat the traffic.
MAMA OLUAKA	*(Shaking her head gleefully in an understanding manner whilst still putting in the first man's order)* My son, I am coming; I have only one hand; I will sell to you; it is first come first served. Give me time to attend to him *(makes a face towards the 1st man) inu.*
2ND MAN	*(Shaking his legs impatiently)* Okay Oh! I will wait.
A LITTLE GIRL	*(Money in hand tugging at Mama Oluaka's wrapper)* Mummy akara, I want to buy akara fifty naira.
MAMA OLUAKA	*(Smiling softly whilst looking towards Oluchi her daughter who is standing with hands across her chest looking at the small crowd that had began to gather)* Oluchi, what are you doing standing there hands across your chest. Come and help me serve our customers will you!
2ND MAN	*(Frowning)* She will not serve me Oh! I believe I have the right to demand who serves me here.
OLUCHI	*(Frowning as she approaches her mother)* You see the reason why I don't like serving your customers when they come? They say I don't serve them as much as you would.

scene 2

2ND MAN *(Not smiling)* And is that a lie? You don't give jara as much as your mum does and each time you come to serve us; you have about you a very unwelcoming face.

OLUCHI *(Not believing her ears, looking straight at the man)* And how I am supposed to serve you? With face all lit up in smile, or would you rather I walk up to you laughing?

MAMA OLUAKA *(Raising her free left hand, she gives Oluchi a slap across the mouth, keeping her from further speech)* Will you shut up your mouth? Is this how you are going to take care of my customers; by running your mouth at anyone that comes your way, ehn?

OLUCHI *(Hands to mouth as she rubs her lips calmly)* Mummy, I am sorry. But I don't like the way they talk...

MAMA OLUAKA *(The index finger of her left finger to her lips* shhh! I will hear no further from you. Will you quickly apologize to my customer?

OLUCHI *(Still rubbing her sore lips, not looking up at the 2nd man)* I am sorry Sir.

MAMA OLUAKA *(Not satisfied)* Is that how I taught you to apologize to your elders?

OLUCHI *(Bending slightly on her knee)* I am very sorry Sir.

MAMA OLUAKA Will you quickly sell to the young girl now *(her left index finger pointing to the*

	little girl)
OLUCHI	*(Going over to the transparent plastic bowl to sell akara to the little girl, head down in submission)* I am sorry Mum *(To the girl):* What do you want?
LITTLE GIRL	*(In a low voice)* Aunty, I want fifty Naira akara.

(Oluchi begins to go through the process of getting at a black polythene bag, getting a fork and piercing the bean balls with the fork and into the polythene bag)

MAMA OLUAKA *(Looking pleadingly at the 2nd man)* Please forgive my daughter; don't mind her words. You know how children of these days are, very quick to use their tongues. Please forgive. *(Begins to put into a black polythene bag the items the man had requested).* Here, have your order *(Extending her hand with the man's orders in the black polythene bag)*

2ND MAN *(Taking the polythene bag while handing her money for the items)* That's the very reason I choose to have you serve me Mama Akara. You are a very down-to-earth woman. Young girls of nowadays have their eyes upward. They do not value work. They believe that once they can speak English as a sign of being educated, that they have arrived.

scene 2

MAMA OLUAKA *(Pleadingly with hands clasped)* It is okay Sir. She won't talk back at you or anyone again. You know these girls. She doesn't even know she is chasing my customers away by her attitude; she forgets it is from the proceeds that I make from the money they give me that I pay her school fees.

2ND MAN *(Beginning to walk away)* Ah! Don't mind them. I have one in my house; my daughter. She has refused to learn a trade. I tell her I am fortunate to have gotten a Civil Service job but that now it is difficult to get a white collar job. I have even told her to learn a skill while waiting to get at a job and she has bluntly refused. You know, when they speak the English Man's language as a show of being educated; they forget that it is no visa to employment.

MAMA OLUAKA *(Heaving a sigh of relief)* It is well Sir. Alright, you have a good day. Please, come again tomorrow Oh!

(2nd Man leaves as a few other customers approach Mama Oluaka. Mama Oluaka begins to attend to them alongside her daughter Oluchi)

(A distance away from MAMA OLUAKA, is FANCY and FLAIR. They both have on loose

	fitting sweat shirts on three quarters jean trousers)
FLAIR	So, this is the place. The seller is the woman over there *(Points towards Mama Oluaka)* you can go there and buy what you want while I go over to this shop *(Pointing towards a shop)* to buy some eggs.
FANCY	*(Wide eyed)* You are asking me to go over there alone to buy bean balls?
FLAIR	*(Heaves a sigh of frustration)* What's wrong with that?
FANCY	*(Pleadingly)* Let's go together please. She's your customer and will give us more jara as you are her customer.
FLAIR	*(Smiling)* So, you love jara ehn?
FANCY	*(Smiling broadly)* Yes! I love free things, so long as they're good. Her bean balls are delicious and well made. Let her give me as many bean balls as she can as jara.
FLAIR:	Funny you; let's go.
	(They walk together towards MAMA OLUAKA who is bidding bye-bye to the last customer and her daughter who is seated on a bench with her arms folded across her chest shielding herself from the early morning cold)
FLAIR	*(All smiles)* Good morning Ma.
FANCY	*(Standing behind FLAIR, in an undertone)* Good morning ma'am.

scene 2

MAMA OLUAKA *(Smiling, eyes fixed on FLAIR, lit with appreciation)* Good morning, my dear, anything for us?
FLAIR Yes Ma. My friend here *(Pointing at Fancy who is currently busy looking around the shaded spot Mama Oluaka occupied)* wants to buy akara. She ate your fries and loved them so much, particularly your bean balls; so she has decided to purchase some today.
MAMA OLUAKA *(Smiling broadly)* Isn't that good news? *Ahia oma na ere onwe ya* my dear. So, how much of what does she want?
FLAIR *(Tapping Fancy lightly on her left side)* How much of bean balls do you need?
FANCY *(Startling from Flair's tap not obviously paying attention to the discourse but on the present surrounding)* Two hundred. I would also need sweet potatoes for one hundred and plantain for fifty.
MAMA OLUAKA *(Smiling)* Does she want sauce to taste?
FLAIR *(Nodding)* Sure she does Ma.
(Mama Oluaka goes about getting at a polythene bag and a fork and begins to pick out the items Fancy had requested.)
FANCY *(Whispering to Flair in a low disapproving tone, while using her left hand as a fan to whisk away flies)* Is this the place you come to buy fries?

FLAIR	*(Indifferent, looking at MAMA OLUAKA as she puts the fries into the polythene bag)* Yes, why?
FANCY	This place isn't real neat, you know?
FLAIR	*(In a low tone not looking at Flair)* Well not as neat as it is in London but neat enough for a middle aged struggling woman who is doing what she knows best to support her family.
FANCY	*(Still whispering)* But couldn't she have secured a more decent stall, or shop to set up this business of hers rather than stick to this shade?
FLAIR	*(Whispering right back):* I think the right question should be, does she have that much money to set up a more decent shop or stall?
FANCY	*(Refraining from whispering as she looks disdainfully at MAMA OLUAKA's right hand as it moved about the plastic bowls getting her orders with the help of the fork)* Oh! No! Take a look at those fingers of hers, all crooked, twisted and rocky-like!
FLAIR	*(Turning to face Fancy heaving a sigh of exasperation)* Would you just let the poor woman alone.
FANCY	*(Sneaky, in a low tone)* Yeah, it's all part of getting to work with ones hands, isn't it? *(Taking up her hands and looking admiringly*

scene 2

                  at her fine fingernails)
(TO HERSELF): Mine are not meant for such tedious, menial work.
(A YOUNG WOMAN with loosely tied wrapper about her chest, with two hundred Naira note in hand walks up to MAMA OLUAKA)
YOUNG WOMAN *(Demandingly)* Mama akara, *i boolachi, biko, nye m* akara fifty naira, potato fifty na plantain fifty. *Biko, osiiso, osiiso. Naani obere nwa m no n'ulo.*
MAMA OLUAKA *(Beckoning on her daughter who is busy peeling the back of a sweet potato to prepare it for frying):* Oly *nwa m,* biko, come and sell to this aunty Oh!

(OLUCHI leaves off peeling the potato and advances towards her mother. She takes the woman's orders again and begins to put her orders into a polythene bag)

OLUCHI *(To the young woman):* Here, aunty, have your order *(Hands her the polythene bag)*
YOUNG WOMAN *(Collects the bag from her)* Here *(gives her the two hundred naira note she had come with)*

(OLUCHI collects the money from her and puts it into her mother's apron and then searches for her change. She finds a fifty naira note, gives it to the customer and reclaims her seat

and continues to peel the sweet potatos)

MAMA OLUAKA *(Watching FANCY from the corner of her eyes) (To FLAIR)* It appears this friend of yours is a been-to.

FLAIR   Yes, she is. She has just returned from London where she was studying for a master's degree.

MAMA OLUAKA: Oh! I see. I've been observing her since you two came here. She seems a bit too pampered.

FLAIR   *(Smiling)* Yes Ma.

MAMA OLUAKA *(Smiling)* How about your bead business?

FLAIR   *(Eyes aflame with interest)* Ma, I am making progress Oh! I just finished making a customer's bag. When would you have me make a bag for you? I believe you need one.

MAMA OLUAKA *(Smiling)* I admire your courage to do something to earn a living rather than wait around for a job. *(Shaking her head as though in thought)* Well, I'll think about it and tell you.

FLAIR   *(Smiling earnestly)* I can't wait to hear from you. I don't charge much.

MAMA OLUAKA *(Extending the nylon containing Fancy's orders towards Flair whose hand is outstretched to collect the bag from MAMA OLUAKA)* Take. Don't worry, when I am ready; I will let you know.

scene 2

FLAIR | *(Collecting the nylon bag)* Okay Ma, thank you. *(Turning to face Fancy)* Here, *(hands her the polythene bag containing the fries.)*
FANCY | *(Collects the polythene bag from her with both hands. She then fishes her hand into her trouser pocket and gets out a five hundred Naira note and hands it to Flair)* Here, give her that.
FLAIR | *(Turning to face MAMA OLUAKA, she extends her right hand holding the note with the support of her left hand to show respect)* Ma, here's your money.
MAMA OLUAKA | *(Collects the money from her and begins to scout through the few notes inside her apron for the change. She gets out a hundred naira note and a fifty naira note and hands them to Flair)* Here, have your balance my daughter; *nwa azulu azu.*
FLAIR | *(Smiling self-consciously)* Oh! Thank you, I am grateful. *Ahia oma.* *(Turning to face Fancy)* Alright, let's get going to the other shop.
FANCY | *(In enthusiasm):* Yes, please let's get going. I can't wait to eat down these fries you see; I want them hot and then again, you know I have to be at the salon later today to have my hair fixed and do some kind of manicure and pedicure.
FLAIR | *(Heaves a sigh)* Yes Ma! *(They begin to walk*

	away briskly from MAMA OLUAKA's shade)
FANCY	*(Smiling)* It appears this woman has an eye for you?
FLAIR	*(Embarrassed)* How do you mean?
FANCY:	Oh! I saw the flicker of light in her eyes the moment she saw you and she just seems to love to hear you speak. And what was that *nwa azulu azu* about?
FLAIR	*(Somewhat resolute)* Oh! Please, spare me some stories this morning.
FANCY	*(Speaking more to herself than to FLAIR in a low tone)* Who knows, she just might be rooting you for one of her sons.
FLAIR	*(Impatient)* I heard that! I perceive you were spoiled with bedtime stories. How do you know she has sons, or even grown up ones at that? Or could it possibly be that your upcoming meeting with your fiancé is making you see blues?
FANCY	*(Smiling wildly)* Yeah, that too. But I know rooting when I see one. Or could it be the mere admiration of your entrepreneurial spirit which she seems also to have?
FLAIR	*(Plainly)* Most assuredly, should be. Could you please hurry up, we need to hurry.
FANCY:	I am walking as fast as I can Flair.
FLAIR	*(Smiling coyly)* Good.

scene 2

(They enter a shop to purchase fresh eggs as light fades)

END OF SCENE 2

SCENE 3

(In the market, at about 8am in the morning.

Several traders dealing in the sale of fruits and vegetables are busy about their selling activities. Some are busy arranging their wares, others are beckoning on customers with either their eyes, hands or calling them names that they dim fit not necessarily names they know the persons called bear. Others are busy counting monies gotten from already concluded sales to be sure their money-maths is correct. Amongst them are buyers haggling prices, touching food items, weighing and sizing them up like they were inspecting bird traps. Some are busy touching food items they know they would not need and were not ready to buy. Others just passed on not paying attention to the winking eyes, nudging hands and endearing words of traders who called ever so endearingly.

Amidst the hundreds of people either buying or selling; MAMA OLUAKA enters the market in her near faded apparels of the day; her apron wrapped to a small size is placed under her left armpit and in her right hand is a blue shopping bag. She advances towards the shop of a trader who

SCENE 3

sells "oha" leaves. In front of the entrance to her shop is a bold inscription "NO CREDIT TODAY; COME TOMORROW". The name of the trader is MADAM HUSTLE. She is seated on a stool in her shop when MAMA OLUAKA enters her shop)

MAMA OLUAKA (Smiling as she approaches the trader) Madam Hustle, good morning, *kee ka i mee?*
MADAM HUSTLE (Smiling as she gets up the stool) Good morning Ma. *A di m nma; A na eme nu, Jehovah bu Eze!*
MAMA OLUAKA (Nodding in acknowledgment) Good morning Ma, I am. *O bu ezie, Jehovah bu Eze.* I want to purchase some oha leaves. *(She walks towards a table in MADAM HUSTLE'S shop whereon are displayed several oha leaves all tied up in bundles and left lying helplessly on the table and begins to lift bundle after bundle up, sizing them, weighing them with both her hands and eyes)*
MADAM HUSTLE (Helping MAMA OLUAKA out by selecting a bundle of oha leaves she considers fuller than others) They are all of very good quality, just two hundred naira a bundle. *Lee nke a,* It's much fuller *(Hands her the bundle of oha leaves)* It is said that good wares sell themselves. I know you know what is good. My oha leaves are fresh; take a look at the sticks; they are red in colour which speaks

of their quality. So, take this bundle of oha that I am giving you.

MAMA OLUAKA *(Looking suspiciously at MADAM HUSTLE)* You are sure that one you have in your hand is fuller than all the others?

MADAM HUSTLE *(Quietly dropping the bundle of oha leaves she has in hand on the table)* Oya, select by yourself, hence you think I am out to cheat you. *(Walking towards her seat to reclaim her sitting position)*

MAMA OLUAKA *(Shaking her head negatively)* No, it's not like that, I just...

MADAM HUSTLE *(Interrupting while sitting)* No, that's the way we market people are. We are cheats; we cheat our customers, those who buy from us; we exact and extort from them; give them rotten vegetables and fruits at high prices. Is it not said, no word of truth proceeds from the mouth of we traders.

MAMA OLUAKA *(Still shaking her head negatively)* No. It has not come to that.

MADAM HUSTLE *(Insisting)* Yes, it has. Turn around, go to the woman over there *(Pointing ahead of MAMA OLUAKA)* go and check out her oha leaves, and afterwards make your choice. *(Begins to beckon on no one in particular)* Your fresh vegetables, your fresh vegetables here, it is me Madam Hustle, I am around,

SCENE 3

please come now for your fresh vegetables. My vegetables are taste and see; a trial will convince you..

MAMA OLUAKA *(bewildered)* Haba! Madam Hustle; don't talk like that. I am a trader like you. But, I don't have to tongue lash my customers before they decide to patronize me. You are my customer; I always buy vegetables from you; the woman of whom you speak, I saw her and her vegetables but I chose to come to your shop, why then would you ask me to go to her shop?

MADAM HUSTLE *(Face down in obvious embarrassment)* I didn't mean it like that Ma. I am sorry; please select whichever bundle of oha you want. I need you to patronize me Ma.

MAMA OLUAKA *(In a reassuring tone)* Please, come and select for me. Only give me very choice ones as I will be using it to prepare oha leaf soup for my son who will be arriving today from the Whiteman's land. He's told me to prepare it for him as it's been long he last had it.

MADAM HUSTLE *(Rises from her sitting position and begins to walk towards Mama Oluaka)* Waoh! In that case; I will be most willing to help. *(Begins to touch and lift several oha leaves to consider which of them felt weightier and looked fresher)* Here, check these *(Hands her two bundles of*

oha leaves)
MADAM HUSTLE *(Lifts and weights two more bundles of oha leaves and hands them over to Mama Oluaka)* Here, have these two.
MAMA OLUAKA *(Collects the bundles from her and keeps them on a section of madam hustle's table, opens her shopping bag and puts the bundles of oha leaves into it; takes out her apron, carefully unfolds it and brings out a thousand naira note and hands it to Madam Hustle)* Here, have your money.
MADAM HUSTLE *(Collects the note from Mama Oluaka with both hands, her knee half bending in appreciation)* Thanks Ma. *(She opens a drawer built into her table and checks for mama Oluaka's balance)* Here is your balance Ma *(Extending her right hand with a two hundred Naira note in it)*
MAMA OLUAKA *(Collects the note)* Thank you and have a good selling time *(Turns to leave)*
MADAM HUSTLE *(Smiling sheepishly)* Oh! Yes Oh! This vegetable selling business has really done me good.
MAMA OLUAKA *(Turning to face her)* Is that right, how so?
MADAM HUSTLE *(Smiling broadly)* Well, from the profit I made from my selling vegetables Ma, I've been able to buy three plots of land at Ndouka Estate area.
MAMA OLUAKA *(Eyes widening in surprise)* Really? That's

SCENE 3

good news! Thank God.

MADAM HUSTLE Yes Oh! Thank you for patronizing me. You are one of those who made it possible. If you hadn't been purchasing from me; how would I have been able to realize sufficient money with which to purchase that land in such a choice area?

MAMA OLUAKA *(Smiling benignly)* Yes, I can only but imagine. But then you sell fresh vegetables; who wouldn't want to purchase from you? Keep the good work up, okay.

MADAM HUSTLE *(Head bowed in humble acceptance)* Thank you Ma, go well and please, come another time.

MAMA OLUAKA *(Turns to go)* Surely!

MADAM HUSTLE *(In a loud tone)* Na Madam Hustle with the fresh vegetables here! Come and buy your own. Your fresh vegetables, your fresh vegetables here, come and buy your fresh, fresh, vegetables here!

MAMA OLUAKA *(Collecting the Bundles from her)* Thank you, I need two more bundles.

(Mama Oluaka walks out of Madam Hustle's shop into the open market and makes to take a left turn when she is intercepted by MADAM ACTION a seller of grains)

MADAM ACTION *(Holding firmly to Mama Oluaka's left hand)* Mama Oluaka come and buy beans from my hand abeg. Today wey I catch you; come and buy; my beans make sense.

MAMA OLUAKA *(Amused)* My dear, I for consider buy your beans; but you see beans still plenty for my house, Mama Action, no worry, next time.

MADAM ACTION *(Jokingly letting go of her hand)* I know say you go talk next time; okay Oh! Well done Mama Oluaka; your akara na one in town; make you keep am up Ma.

MAMA OLUAKA *(With a grateful smile)* Thank you my dear. If say no be you and your pikin them wey dey buy from my hand, what I for do? Thank you for patronizing quality; thank you for patronizing me.

MADAM ACTION *(Gradually withdrawing)* You are welcome. We dey envy you Oh! You dey work hard well, well. Na your early mor mor wake up for to sell akara make me self kuku stand up for my feet begin hustle Oh! Every morning as you commot market na so, so my husband go dey use you show me sample. If to say my husband no dey ring am like bell for my ears say make I find something begin do make I for help am with bringing money for house; if to say he no dey tell me say make I look you say, upon say you old pas me wella, you still dey commot early mor mor dey come find wetin you go do take care of family, ehn; I

SCENE 3

for still dey quarrel with am today for sake say the money wey him dey give me no dey do for us to chop for house. So, i dey thank you wella Mama Akara for say you show me good example, say woman suppose work to helep family. Thank you very much.

MAMA OLUAKA *(Stretching out her hands)* i dey show my daughter, i dey show; you never see where my hard work show himself? i dey show himself for my hands and my fingers; my bent, curved, distorted; stiffened, wry, contorted fingers *(near tears)* na for sake of pikin them.

MADAM ACTION *(In a knowing look)* No worry mama na; you go reap the fruits of your labour. *Aka aja aja na ebute onu nmanu nmanu!* No be so unaa dey talk am?

MAMA OLUAKA *(Wipes the little tears that had formed at the sides of her eyes)* Na so, amin!

(She begins to make a graceful walk out of the spot she was standing when she is roughly jerked to a side by a group of young men running along her path of walk)

1ST YOUTH   Catch him! Catch him! Thief! Thief! Thief!
2ND YOUTH   He is getting away, catch him! Run faster! *(The market is rowdy as a few young men engage in intense running towards a particular direction)*

MAMA OLUAKA *(Recovering from the jerking and speaking*

to no one in particular) What is going on, who stole what?

A MARKET WOMAN *(Responding to Mama Oluaka's statement)* I suspect that they have caught a thief and you know the market boys; they will beat hell out of him and then set him ablaze.

MAMA OLUAKA *(Amazed)* Set who ablaze? *(Begins to half-run towards the direction the young men had ran to shouting)* Stop! Stop!
(She comes upon some boys who were beating up the supposed thief) Stop! What do you think you are doing?

(The men do not listen as their shouts of 'kill him', 'set him on fire', 'thief', 'onye ori' 'teach him a lesson' deafened Mama Oluaka's words.)

MAMA OLUAKA *(Wriggling her way through the small crowd to the centre of the group and shouting at the top of her voice)* Stop my sons, stop!

1ST YOUTH *(An average height dark complexioned youth with very muscular arms gotten either from carrying weights or from carrying loads and doing very tedious physical activity angrily jerking the thief by the collar with his right hand while other youths momentarily stop their beating of him)*: Our mother, why are you interfering with our affair eh?

MAMA OLUAKA *(Appealing)* My children do not deal so wickedly, eh. What has he done to deserve this

SCENE 3

	beating from you all? *(Looking at each of them squarely in the face)*
1ST YOUTH	*(Looking Mama Oluaka up and down in disdain)* Ah! Ah! Kee ihe nma anyi a na akogheri, eh? i nuru na nmadu zuru ori i na a ju kee ihe omee *(His free left hand to his ears)* Nti oshiri gi, enwere ihe na eme gi na nti?
2ND YOUTH	*(Agitated and pacing about)* Mama, this young man stole two sophisticated phones from our GSM Chairman Gburugburu and stealthily walked away thinking we would not detect it, but we are smart na, so we detected it and gave him a hot chase and now here he is. He shall face our wrath and judgment today.
ALL YOUTH	*(In one voice)* Yes!
1ST YOUTH	(With rage in his eyes): And no one will be able to stop us!
ALL YOUTH	*(In one voice)* Yes!
MAMA OLUAKA	*(In desperation)* But you have retrieved your Chairman's gadgets from him, haven't you?
1ST YOUTH	*(Fuming and shaking his head questioningly while pushing the culprit about by the collar)* Yes, we have and so?
MAMA OLUAKA	*(Appealing)* If that is the case my son then please let this young man go eh. See what pain, injuries, you have already inflicted on

	him. It should be enough.
1ST YOUTH	*(Shaking his head in the negative while still shaking the thief's neck here and there as he jerks him fiercely by the collar)* Who is this woman? *Biko, onye malu nwanyi a kpopu ya ebea kitaa tupu m mawa ya anya.*
2ND YOUTH	*(Shaking his head disapprovingly)* No. You don't talk to an elderly woman like that Obike. It's rude. I will not accept of it.
1ST YOUTH	*(Motioning with his free left hand)* Then, take her out of here while I do my job *(beginning to beat the thief harshly on his head with his left hand)*
2ND YOUTH	*(To Mama Oluaka appealingly)* Mama please leave this place. These young men will not hear you and they can hurt you in order to carry out their verdict on the thief.
MAMA OLUAKA	*(Resolute)* No. He will have to deal with me first. *(To the 1st Youth)* This young man you and your fellow thugs are beating up, is he the first to steal, are you and your thugs free from theft? The story is rife of some errand boys, some shop attendants, trainees who stealthily make away with their masters' money, property without their knowledge. If any one of you has been guilty of stealing why are you quick to take the life of another who has stolen simply because

SCENE 3

1ST YOUTH	you caught him, ehn? *(Chest heaving in obvious rage)* Silas, kpopu this old woman here. *(Moves forcefully towards Mama Oluaka in order to forcefully push her away leaving the collar of the thief's shirt momentarily, but he is intercepted by the 2nd Youth)*
2ND YOUTH	*(Standing in his way)* Obike, don't be unnecessarily rude; this woman is old enough to be your mother; you should give her a listening ear.
1ST YOUTH	*(Pointing threateningly at Silas)* Make you take this woman commot here make I do my job.
2ND YOUTH	*(Beginning to get irritated)* And what exactly is your job, to carry out jungle justice on supposed thieves?
1ST YOUTH	*(Forcefully, jerks Silas away and pushes Mama Oluaka out of the circle; he turns backwards and makes to pound on the thief who is left at the mercy of other youths who have been dormant all the while doing nothing but stare at and listen to the tirade of words between the two youths and Mama Oluaka)* Come here, you thief, you must die *(Gives him some tirades of blows while the other youths keep the thief from fleeing by forming a circle)* You, you, go die here today *(Turns*

	to the idle youths) Go and get me a tire and kerosene quickly.
2ND YOUTH	*(Recovering from the jerk, he advances towards Obike and pulls him violently away from the thief)* Stop what you are doing!
MAMA OLUAKA	*(Half runs towards Silas and begins to persuade him her nylon and apron bags dangling about her in the act)* Stop my son, stop.
1ST YOUTH	*(Staggers and quickly recovers, turns and advances towards Silas)* i be like say you wan suffer with this thief abii. I go show you pepper now.
	(He begins to pull his shirt in order to prepare for a thorough fight and while he is yet at it, three men in police uniform arrive the scene. They, without recourse to anyone rush into the crowd, whisk the said thief away and begin their frantic march towards a Hilux van parked not too far from the spot the crowd had gathered.)
2ND YOUTH	*(Smiling benignly)* Very good, you go kill your father if you want.
1ST YOUTH	*(Glaring angrily about on discovering after pulling his shirt that the police had whisked his prey away)* You *(Advancing towards the 2nd Youth bare-chested)* It's your fault.
2ND YOUTH	*(Making himself available to the 1st Youth)* How Obike, how?

SCENE 3

MAMA OLUAKA *(Coming in between them)* Do not cause a raucous my dears. Stop this already.

1ST YOUTH *(Pointing the index finger of his left hand at her)* Nwanyi a si ebe a pua kitaa!

2ND YOUTH *(Quietly taking Mama Oluaka aside)* Mama, leave this guy, He does not hear smooth language *(Facing 1st Youth)* Obike do your worst.

(1st Youth makes to advance towards the 2nd Youth when he is caught off guard by five young men who quickly enclose him)

3RD YOUTH *(A dark complexioned middle aged youth, very tall, with very muscular arms with the popular 'dada' hair for which mad men are known, in black three quarters trousers, fuming)* Obike, o di ka ara na agba gi. A no m ebea a na agwa gi hapu this old woman aka. i ka na ezuzughari. Kee ife na eme gi n' isi? I na awi ala ehn?

1ST YOUTH *(Perplexed and embarrassed as he recomposes himself)* I am loyal Sir. Oga Cle. *(Bows the knees in respect)* I am very loyal Sir.

3RD YOUTH *(Ordering, index finger of left hand pointing towards the 1st Youth's shirt lying helplessly on the ground)* Ngwa, tutulu efe gi si ebea Pua, now!

1ST YOUTH *(Moves quickly towards his shirt in utmost regard for the intruder)*: All correct Sir. *(Picks*

	up his shirt and begins to walk hastily away into the crowd)
3RD YOUTH	*(Turning to face Mama Oluaka, palms together, appealing)* Please forgive my boy Ma. You know when they finish taking this weed that they take; they forget that not everybody is their mate. Please, forgive him.
MAMA OLUAKA	*(Managing a smile)* Thank you my dear for intervening, and not to worry, I have nothing against him or anyone. It is a good thing the police have taken the young man they were beating away. I was only sacred for his life. Do you know what it means to take the life of another? *(Exhales sharply as she begins to take a graceful walk out of the area)* Have a nice day *umu m (To the 2nd Youth, smiling)* You be a good boy, Oh!
2ND YOUTH	*(Head bowed in submission)* Yes Ma. *(Mama Oluaka and some of the youths who had gathered leave the arena leaving behind the 2nd Youth, 3rd youth and a male trader)*
MALE TRADER	*(Questioningly)* Na male thief or female thief dem catch?
2ND YOUTH	Why are you asking?
MALE TRADER	Haba, I wasn't here to see the show na that's why I am asking; abii is it a crime to ask questions?
2ND YOUTH	The issue is not that you are asking questions;

SCENE 3

                    but what kind of question you are asking oga Linus?
MALE TRADER Wetin do the question wey I ask?
2ND YOUTH Oga Li, you dey ask whether na male abii female dem catch.
MALE TRADER *(Smiling mischievously)* You be man na, you suppose know every na
2ND YOUTH *(Submitting)* Na male Oh! Make you no dey think otherwise
MALE TRADER *(Beginning to make gestures excitedly)* Ah! if na female, *i manu, aga epugodi nu uzo gbaa ya oto ka anyi nwee ike i kiri i manu...*
3RD YOUTH *(Interrupts in a forceful tone)* Taa, meshie gi onu. Have some self respect. *Lee o dika okwu si gi n'onu na aputa.*
MALE TRADER *(Abruptly tightening his face)* Oga Cletus, you be man like me Oh! No dey talk to me like that Oh!
2ND YOUTH *(Impatient)* Oga Linus, stop abeg.
3RD YOUTH *(Not moved by Linus' words)* A na ekwu okwu ihe bara uru, i na ako ihe na agba ka moto. Taa meshie gi onu. Is that how sensible men talk?
MALE TRADER *(Straightening himself and making a salute)* Yes Sir! My mouth is sealed Sir.
3RD YOUTH *(Smiling as he walks towards the male trader and extends his right hand to him for a shake)* Nnaa my man, *kee kwanu?*

MALE TRADER (*Smiling broadly as he accepts his hand in a shake*) Onweghi di. Kee maka ndi a?
3RD YOUTH   Ha no ya.
MALE TRADER This stealing every time don too much Oh! Oga Cletus.
2ND YOUTH   Na government dey cause am Oh!
MALE TRADER No employment, no jobs, why stealing and robbery no go increase?
3RD YOUTH   (*Shakes his head disapprovingly*) It is not only the fault of the government; it is also the fault of the citizens. Must everybody have a white collar job; must everybody be gainfully employed; must everyone be employed by the government?
MALE TRADER (*Heaves a sigh*) Everybody mustn't my brother but...
3RD YOUTH   (*Interrupts*) But what?
MALE TRADER (*Making a face*) Wetin government do about providing jobs?
2ND YOUTH   (*Agreeing*) Oga Linus, please ask oga Cletus.
3RD YOUTH   (*Reasoning as he shakes his head from side to side*) If the government has failed to do something about providing jobs for her citizens; then citizens should do something about jobs in order to survive. They can create jobs. Abii no be trader you be? (*Glaring Linus in the face*)
MALE TRADER (*Nodding in acceptance*) Na trader I be but

SCENE 3

3RD YOUTH	me no go school now. I no pass standard six. Yes! That's what I am saying. You knew you would not fit into a white collar job and you did something about it eh. You chose to trade, not so?
MALE TRADER	*(Further nodding in acceptance although sceptical about what point Cletus was trying to make)* Yes, but...
3RD YOUTH	*(Nodding vehemently)* Yes and so in the same vein even though I am a graduate and I do not immediately find a job doing; I should do something about my unemployed state.
2ND YOUTH	*(Perplexed)* Something like what Sir; something like going around the market picking some items at wholesale price and reselling them abii?
3RD YOUTH	And what is wrong with that eh, Silas, what? You see, it is this 'I have arrived', this 'I am too big for this kind of work' mentality and attitude of ours that has kept us down. What is wrong with picking up some clothes in a certain cheap market and reselling those clothes with little extras as gain elsewhere? *(The 2ND Youth is quiet. He just stands and looks straight ahead)*
MALE TRADER	*(Clears his throat)* Eh! Oga Cletus, you are making sense Oh! *Mana enwekwaranu ka ya bu ihe di, eh. Kedu ka nmadu ga e ji gachaa*

	mahadum puta bido bughariwa carton gala na park na ere ma o bu na e mixieri simenti na building site, eh? o kwesiri ekwesi, eh. oga Cletus?
2ND YOUTH	If only the government were to empower us with jobs, internet fraud acts, bank raiding, credit card swindling, ritual killings for the sole purpose of wealth acquisition would have been reduced to the barest minimum. Is it not with what knowledge these tech guys have garnered that they work mischief? If they had been employed, chances are that they wouldn't have to use what knowledge they have negatively.
2ND YOUTH	*(Shaking his head in disapproval) Asi, onye ori bu onye ori. Oso gi nye ye ten million, o so gi nye ye twenty, o ga na ezu ori. O na adi na obara, hoo, haa!* Based on this, anyone who though educated engages in such acts as fraudulent acts cannot claim it is because the government failed to secure jobs for him that he does so. The person only revealed his evil nature, simple! True, government has not empowered us, but we can empower ourselves by using our brains, working with our hands, creating things from our ideas. *(2nd youth heaves a sigh of desperation and looks about him helplessly)*

SCENE 3

So, if the government does not provide jobs for her citizens; the citizens should create jobs and ask the government to support, empower them. Go to China, children between ages eight and ten are already producing things for sale. They are so entrepreneurial minded; no wonder their country's economy is growing.

MALE TRADER Well, you don win the argument oga Cle. However, me fa, I no go ever accept say make my pikin dem wey do wel for school say make dem follow me enter market begin sell something. If na like that, wetin be the use of the certificate wey dem give them for school?

3RD YOUTH It's not all about trading in the market. There's need for skill acquisition. He/she can choose to make good use of what knowledge he/she has acquired to produce things for others' use or consumption. Most of the teachings done at the university, are they not basically theoretical without the best use of practice? So, anyone who out of what theoretical knowledge he/she garners gets to put his/her hands to work at something and produces something new, boom! That person is made!

MALE TRADER You are making sense; but...

3RD YOUTH You are still 'butting' ehn, after all my

explanations. No wonder our dear country keeps getting worse. See eh, in the end, it's all about the money. You are a trader, you are making your money; I am a car dealer, I am making my money; my young man here is a phone repairer; he is making his money and the banker is handling finances; he is making his money. But staying at home, sitting down doing nothing does not make money.

MALE TRADER You are right!

2ND YOUTH But still government has to do something about employment, haba! No wonder the rate of people leaving Nigeria for other nations is on the increase. Have you not heard stories of well read people, professionals in many fields going abroad seeking greener pastures instead of staying back here and developing the nation, why? Is it not because they have no jobs or are underpaid here? *Enwere onye na abu etinye ya nmanu anu na onu o si enye ya agbailu eh?*

3RD YOUTH *(Acknowledging)* Yes, some of our most gifted, talented and educated persons have left the country to other countries seeking greener pastures; but what about those of them who left without the slightest skill, education, eh? *inubeghi akuko banyere umunne anyi*

SCENE 3

                    no obodo oyibo ndi ihe ha na aru bu ibu nshi, ilekota ndi mere okenye, ma obu ilekotara ndi ocha umu ha eh? Kedu udi nkpari di nke ahu, onye oburu nshi, eh? Yet our brothers still do it for the money. They send down money here for us to use in buying lands and building houses for them; yet such monies were gotten from doing jobs considered unacceptable, odd. If they can do such odd jobs for the money; why can't we, ehn?

2ND YOUTH   Oga Cletus, you are making sense Oh!

MALE TRADER *(Nodding in acceptance)* Yes Oh!

                    (A young fair complexioned boy of about ten years comes upon them. He has on a three quarters blue jeans and a yellow polo. He doesn't look too well. He walks towards the 3rd Youth. He is ABILITY by name.)

ABILITY   *(To Male Trader and 2nd Youth)* Uncle good morning Sir

BOTH   Good morning Ability.

ABILITY   *(To 3rd Youth)* Daddy, daddy *(Tapping him lightly on his left thigh)*

3RD YOUTH   Yes, what is it Ability? Do you want me to buy biscuit for you? You want a soft drink?

ABILITY   *(Ability shakes his head in the negative)* No daddy

MALE TRADER This one wey you carry your son come market,

3RD YOUTH	all well? My brother, he no well Oh! I come tell am say make he follow me come work so I go take care of am. Him mama do small travel with the other smaller ones na im make i say make i carry am come shop.
MALE TRADER	*(Shaking his head to show sympathy)* Okay, Ability sorry, you hear.
	(Ability nods his head in acceptance)
2ND YOUTH	Sorry Oh! Ability.
	(Ability nods his head in acceptance)
ABILITY	*(To 3rd Youth)* Daddy, someone wants to buy a car; he said to call you.
3RD YOUTH	*(Beginning to leave the other two in the company of his son)* Alright my people let me go and do the day's job. My family's sustenance depends on it.
MALE TRADER	*(Acknowledging)* You are right my brother, let me get to work myself *(He begins to leave in a different direction)*
2ND YOUTH	Me too *(He begins his walk towards another direction as Light fades.)*

END OF SCENE 3

SCENE 4

Afternoon, at about 2pm In MAMA OLUAKA'S bedroom, a lavishly coloured sizeable room of lilac and purple with a king-sized bed having on top of it flashy, expensive bags and head gears of different colours. Littered about the floor of her room which is covered in very thick blue carpet are slipper-shoes and high-heeled shoes of diverse colours. She is currently standing before a mirror tying and retying her expensive ashoke about her waist. On her head is an auto-gele, peach in colour. Her blouse, decked in Peruvian beads is also peach in colour and so also is her ashoke wrapper. Her face is covered in very thick foundation powder concealing her wrinkles, few freckles and other facial blemishes. Her ears have long dangling gold earrings on them and her lips glowed from the smear of a red lip stick.

On her feet, she has on high-heeded black sandals. About her left wrist is a gold-plated wrist watch from Calvin-Klein. She sings Donna Summer's 'She Works Hard for the Money' as she ties and re-ties her wrapper.

MAMA OLUAKA *(Shaking her frail waist from side to side while* *nodding in acceptance to the wordings of her song)* She works hard for the money, so hard for the money; she works hard for the money, so you better treat her right. *(Begins to hum the lyrics of the song as she carefully checks her facial makeover in the mirror)* Girl, don't you look real young and pretty today? *(Pats her face slowly with the palm of her right hand as she smiles into the mirror)* Thanks Oly my dear for this makeover. Look how young I look in it. The world is really changing. *(Heaves a sigh of relief)*: A na amagide uwa joorji.

(In a high pitch): Chukwunakwugwoolu! *(Louder)*: Chukwunakwuugwuo! *(Near Screaming)* Nakwuugwo! Reward!

REWARD a handsome well shaven man of about twenty five enters Mama Oluaka's room dressed in corporate black pants and white short sleeved shirt tucked neatly into his pants, a car key in hand. He is Mama Oluaka's second son, an Engineer.)

REWARD   *(In a somewhat gloomy face)*: Mum!

MAMA OLUAKA *(Agitating as she searches frantically through the piles of bags and head gears on her bed for a bag of matching colour to her attire)*: Are you ready? We are running late for the airport you know.

SCENE 4

REWARD *(Taken aback)* Oh! Come on now, look whose complaining. Who has been waiting for the other this past half hour, you or me?
MAMA OLUAKA *(Agreeing)* You're right my son. I have been the one delaying. You know us women and fashion; I need to look good you know so that your brother will be proud of me when he sees me at the airport eh! Do you want me to follow you to the airport looking all shabby? Was it not because I wasn't well dressed that you nearly disapproved of my coming to your matriculation ceremony few years ago? I have learnt my lesson now. I work for the money; so, I have to take care of myself with my money. If I had told you that the reason why I couldn't afford to wear the expensive clothes you saw other people's mothers wear was because I used the money I could have used to purchase those outlandish clothing to pay your school fees; would you have believed me? *(Still busy ransacking her bed, checking out bags)*
REWARD *(In a remorseful look)* Mum *(In a low tone)* I would and I did. I was and am sorry. But, mum. You know now, who would feel proud of his mum in rags? Mum, you're beautiful. I felt and feel pain seeing you dressed in

clothes that do not accentuate your beauty.

MAMA OLUAKA *(Smiling but not looking up)* Yeah, right. After giving me rags to wear in exchange for your school fees.

REWARD *(Looking his mum over)* Mum, you're dressed gorgeously I must say.

MAMA OLUAKA *(Looking at him for the first time, smiling)* Well, thanks. I have to look good for you young men.

REWARD *(Overly pleased at his mums looks)* Waoh! Mum, you look great. Who made you up?

MAMA OLUAKA I am flattered; your sister did this to me before going for extra mural classes. *(Stressing)* It's called makeover.

REWARD *(Beginning to make exaggerated expressions to pass his point across)* Oh! Mum, you look spritistic! cocastic, fantastic! Fantabulous! Oly is a pro!

MAMA OLUAKA *(Laughing humorously as she frantically searches for an appropriate bag; she finds one and whisks the bag at him)*: Shush, get running so we don't get too late to the airport. You know your elder brother; he'd start fussing all over me for being late.

REWARD *(Cheerful)* Alright mum *(Extending his right hand towards his mum's hand bag to help her with it)* May I help you with that?

MAMA OLUAKA *(Playfully knocks off his extended right*

SCENE 4

                  hand) No. I can very well carry about my own bag.

ENGR. REWARD   *(Turns sharply towards the door)* Yes Ma'am. *(Beginning to walk away)* Let's get going mum and please don't shout when I exceed 80km per hour. We are late and you know that.

MAMA OLUAKA *(Hurriedly following after him)* You dare not Reward *nwa m*. You dare not drive above 80km per hour. Instead, count me out of this journey.

(She keeps hurrying after him as Light fades.)

END OF SCENE 4

SCENE 5

It is about 3pm in the afternoon.

Fancy and Flair are in a salon, with the inscription LOOKING GOOD IS GOOD BUSINESS written boldly in the front of the salon. The salon is stuffed with all kinds of skin, hair, manicure, pedicure and lady-care related products, gadgets hanging about the wall of the salon. In some parts of the wall, big posters of ladies wearing different hair dos, having on artificial eyelashes and well painted fingers and toes nails are arrayed.

Fancy is currently having manicure done on her finger nails by the beautician, DAME who owns the beauty shop while Flair who accompanied her to the salon looks on. There are other attendants in the shop - males and females who are busy braiding, fixing, washing or twisting people's hair or making people over.

FLAIR	*(Admiring Fancy's hairdo)* Fanny, you look great in this hair!
FANCY	*(Excited as she flaunts her newly braided hair*

SCENE 5

	*left and right)*Thanks best friend. It's all for Bent!
FLAIR	*(Cheerful)* Oh! Yeah.
DAME	*(To Flair)* Your friend dey wed?
FLAIR	*(Smiling broadly)* Soon Dame, soon.
DAME	*(Smiling mischievously as she points the nail polish in her right hand at Fancy)* In that case I will give you a great makeover. You just trust me. *(Fancy giggles)*
FLAIR	*(Smiling while being somewhat serious as she points at the beautician)* Yes, please give her an amazing makeover, but I hope you will not cut off her head with your high price; I know you.
DAME	*(Making emphasis with her head as she continues to take care of Fancy's finger nails)* Better soup na money kill am na. I don look this ya friend well, she look like person wey carry better money. Abii no be the person wey wan marry am she wan go see? She suppose dey sharp na so that when he see am, if he want, he go eat am *(Laughs wildly nearly falling over the stool she is sitting on, but she recovers quickly).*
FLAIR	*(Putting forward her hands quickly to hold Dame from falling, laughing)* See where you for fall for ground where you dey

	talk.
FANCY	*(To Flair, a little embarrassed)* This beautician of yours talks foul.
FLAIR	*(Agreeing)* Don't they all?
DAME	*(Preparing for gossip as she inquires)* So, your guy, where's he from; what does he do?
FANCY	*(Becoming a bit protective and surprised at the same time)* And why are you asking?
DAME	*(Serious)* It's nothing personal. *(Lifts up her left fingers to show her wedding ring)* Hello, I am a married woman. It's not that I am man hunting; it's all in the spirit of womanship.
FANCY	*(Easing off a bit)* He's a local; a medical doctor based abroad.
DAME	*(Amused)* Waoh! So, you will be a doctor's wife soon.
FANCY	*(Smiling)* Yes. I can't wait.
DAME	*(Pressing)* He must be reeling of money.
FLAIR	*(Serious)* Stop poking your nose about people's affairs, Dame!
DAME	*(Not minding)* She may choose not to answer abii na you I dey ask?
FANCY	*(Trying to sound casual)* Well he's doing what he can.
DAME	*(Still prying)* Most doctors are hardly free; do you like the idea? They are nearly always busy, the reason why I refused to marry one who had asked my hand in marriage at the

SCENE 5

	time.
FANCY	*(Smiling)* Who likes to have her man around all the time anyway? I know I don't. Let him just get the money rolling in I should be okay with that. And when we are together, we can make up for the times he is busy and away.
DAME	Typical *(Turning to Flair)* Do you like the idea?
FLAIR	*(Exhales air slowly)* Well, it depends. I think I would prefer a man who is less busy so he can find time to be with his family.
DAME	*(In exasperation)* It depends; you think? Anyway, why am I even asking you? You are not in a relationship, so, how would you really know?
FLAIR	*(Defensive)* Dame, don't start. I am not ready for your tirade of words this afternoon, please. You just hurry up and get Fanny's makeover done with so she can go see her fiancé.
DAME	*(Feigning serious)* Yes Ma! I will be done with your friend's make up before you know it. *(Looking at her keenly)* I think I need to make you over lightly, I know you are not the heavy makeup type.
FLAIR	*(A smile spreading across her face)* Hmm, Dame. Leave me alone. I am not going on a date. Do all you can to ensure yours truly *(Pointing at Fancy)* Looks great today, okay.
DAME	*(Acknowledging)* I will do as you have

	requested, but are you not going in the company of your friend to see her guy? If yes, then I need to do some finishing touches on your face before you go; make you no go fall ya friend hand for there.
FANCY	*(Bewildered)* Who? You said who is following me? Stories of girlfriends snatching their girlfriends' guys are rife these days. I will be going solo. You want Flair with her height and gait to steal Bent from me, right?
	(Dame and Flair laugh merrily)
FLAIR	I am not rooting for a medical personnel Fanny! Talk about Entrepreneurs, Business Moguls, Estate Surveyors, Engineers. Right now, I am not ready to be in a relationship. I desire to be financially capable first.
DAME	*(Perplexed)* Did I hear you say you want to be financially capable first?
FLAIR	*(Excitedly)* Yes!
FANCY	*(Disapproving)* Because you are a man, right?
DAME	*(Bewildered)* My dear, I wonder Oh! Make unaa see my customer Oh!
FANCY	The thing is, you have not yet found a man you love; if you do, all these stories of yours would not hold water.
DAME	Gbam!
FLAIR	*(Coming to terms)* Yeah, you may be right about your statement Fancy, but until we

SCENE 5

	meet; I will be doing all I can to be financially capable; it is needful in today's world.
FANCY	There's an Economist here, remember *(Pointing at herself)*: I studied Economics not you. So, come on!
DAME	Flair could be right! I work to augment my husband's income because I know his income cannot make ends meet in our home.
FLAIR	*(Hands spread apart)* You see!
DAME	*(A bit concerned)* Yes. But then my husband is not happy about it.
FANCY	*(Eyes rolling)* You see!
FLAIR	(Surprised) And why is that?
DAME	Well, he is one of those who believes that a woman's role should be in the kitchen and you know what, I agree with him but then what nairas he brings in hardly meet our needs as a family; so I decided to do this *(Points about her salon with the nail polish in her right hand)* to support him and he is mad about it.
FLAIR	*(Eyes widened)* And he would rather you manage with less than enough and stay in the kitchen; how so?
DAME	*(Heaves a sigh)* My dear. It is well. I have stood my ground Oh! I will keep doing this to assist him and to think that what I am doing is something I am passionate about. I mean

	even if it wasn't bringing in money for me; I would still love to do it.
FLAIR	*(Excited)* That's the way to go girl! Doing something you are passionate about and making a living out of it is the way to go. Don't you worry; he'll come around soon. Who doesn't want some easing off the shoulder huh?
FANCY	*(Giving Flair a disapproving look)* I know you would approve. Madam bead bag making.
FLAIR	I love what I do girl *(beaming with a smile)* *(Her phone rings and she picks it and puts it to her left ear)* Hello, who am I onto? Yes. Yes. Really? Are you serious? Oh! Thank you so much ma'am. *(Fancy makes faces at her in a not-too-serous-way)* Are you serious? *(Jumps up the seat she had been sitting on)* Oh! Thank you so very much Ma. Okay. When do I come for the samples? Okay, tomorrow then. Have a nice day ma'am. *(Puts the phone down and looks about her at Fancy and Dame)* Guess what ladies?
BOTH	What?
FLAIR	*(Looking at Fancy)* My customer whom I delivered the bag to before we came here

SCENE 5

	has linked me to another person who has requested that I make three beaded bags for her; she's requested I come over to her house to get samples of the kinds of bag she would have me produce with beads tomorrow.
DAME	*(Excited)* Girl, you are beginning to make waves with this bead making skill of yours. Perhaps you will have to make one for me; I would like you to make me a black beaded bag with a colourless bead mix. Who knows perhaps pretty shortly people will be on the demand for it as the reigning women bag item *(Shrugs her shoulders)* I better have one now that obtaining it is pretty cheap as per obtaining it via a customer *(Winks at Flair smiling)*
FLAIR	*(Super excited as she takes Dames's right hand with the nail polish in it)* Please patronize me; I will not cut off your head with a high price as you do mine.
	(Dame and Flair laugh)
DAME	If I had cut off your head with high prices as you claim you shouldn't have any head by now, should you?
	(both Flair and Dame laugh with mirth but Fancy is withdrawn)
FANCY	*(Changing the topic)* I do not really like the idea of skill acquisition. As a graduate, I mean

DAME   what do I need it for?
          (Putting herself together from the moments of laughter) Well, I believe some people are not cut out for any kind of menial work. So, if the white collar job suits them, then why not, let them go ahead.
FANCY   *(Excited)* Exactly!
FLAIR   *(Sober)* White collar jobs are good and attractive but then, where one does not have access to such jobs; what would one do, idle away?
DAME   *(Facing Fancy's nails to give them a thorough finish)* My dear, you are saying something important there Oh!
          (Gets up from finishing with taking care of Fancy's finger nails and walks towards her dresser table and begins to get items for the makeover she intends to perform on Fancy)
          I mean I know of someone who kept waiting for a job for five years; she literally applied for jobs everywhere she heard and read of but was not lucky. In the end she had to start dealing in the sale of clothes. Today, if you see her boutique you will marvel. I doubt that the white collar job she had been haunting for would have been sufficient to give her the kind of money she makes from her cloth sale business; above all she has time for herself

SCENE 5

	and her family, you know; she's her own boss.
FLAIR	*(With keen interest)* Yeah!
FANCY	*(Shrugs her shoulders)* Each to his own. I am not cut out for that kind of thing, business is not my thing.
DAME	*(Beginning to apply facial powder to Fancy)* My dear, I guess you are only saying this because you are working. I mean think about it. If it happens to be your husband who has to keep bringing in money, chances are that sometimes he would go overboard. And given the current economy, it is only wise that both parties work to secure the future of their children. I mean how many families nowadays have just one person bringing in the money. Such a man would have stress enough and honestly may crash sooner than later.
FANCY	*(Adamant)* No! My Bent will not crash.
DAME	*(Stopping the application of the puff powder as she gives Fancy a good look):* You are not working?
FANCY	No, I'm not; why is that?
DAME	Please don't subscribe to the housewife fairytales Oh! You are a graduate, aren't you?
FLAIR	*(Keenly)* A Master Degree holder.
DAME	*(Beginning to draw her eyebrows)* Nne, wake up Oh!

FANCY	I don't understand you both. I mean are you not the one who just said your husband is mad at you for choosing to do work alongside him?
DAME	Yes. But I did also say his income isn't enough to keep our home up and running.
FANCY	And if his income was to be sufficient and he wouldn't want you to work?
DAME	*(Shrugging her shoulders whilst still doing her job on Fancy's face)*: That perhaps would have been a different ball game altogether.
FANCY	*(Raising her right hand questioningly)* So?
DAME	But you have to know the reality of the day. Money is never enough. With the increase in the money come also the increase in needs and the number of mouths to feed on it as well as your taste. And I can see you are a fashion conscious woman. I will advise you consider working. Well, except of course your man doesn't want you to work and wouldn't mind bearing the brunt of catering for the family. Anyway, you said he lives abroad; certainly things are far better there than there are here.
FLAIR	Dame, you leave my friend alone. Stop lecturing her Oh! She will definitely get a job over there and start working once she settles in. so, please, stop lecturing already.

SCENE 5

FANCY	*(Tired of the two)* You two are obnoxious, God! *(Her phone rings and on seeing the name displayed on the screen of her phone, she sits upright stopping Dame's work on her face abruptly)* Hello Honey! Yeah! Are you candid? Oh! Good gracious! I'm so pleased to hear from you, I missed you a great deal Darling. Where? Could you please text me the location? Welcome back honey. I'll be right about there any moment though I am still at the salon somewhere around Haduani. Alright, I'll be right there soon. *(Drops the phone from her ears excitedly)* My fiancé is back and is requesting to see me *(To Dame)* Could you please hurry up with this makeover of yours please?
DAME	Oh! Yes I will *(Begins to hasten the makeover process)* I will ensure you look adorable today so you can hire me to make you up on your wedding day.
FANCY	*(Shrieks a bit as Dame's fingers touch her face)* Gosh your fingers are so rocky and look so discoloured.
DAME	*(Stops her work as she looks her fingernails and palms over)* Yes, you're right. These are the signature of what I am doing for a living. The caustic relaxers which I use to perm my customers' hair; their caustic hair dyes,

	conditioners and hair treatments play their roles on my palms and fingers.
FANCY	Well, you could have used gloves; I mean those have a function they do right?
DAME	*(Still looking down at her palms and fingers)* Yes I should have but they are not always handy and sometimes; time is of the essence, I may not even remember to put them on *(Smiles)*
FLAIR	*(To Dame, interrupting, as she taps her lightly on the left shoulder)* Hurry up Dame, she shouldn't be late; you know how Haduani area is with the traffic.
DAME	*(Resumes work on Fancy's face)* I was doing it as quickly as I could until your friend decided to pick at my palms and fingers. Shebi if i no do am well now, unaa go talk say i make am look like wili-wili.
FLAIR	*(Half-smiling)* Dame. You are good at what you do. So, I know that even in haste, you will do a great job.
DAME	*(Making finishing touches)* There, look yourself in the mirror.
FANCY	*(Getting up the chair as she heads towards a mirror in the salon; excited)* Oh! I like what I see. *(Turns to face Dame)* You've done a great job; thanks.
	(Dame smiles and looks down at her palms)

SCENE 5

	(Fancy walks towards the chair she had just gotten up from and lifts up her black Givenchy bag which sat beside the chair; she takes out her purse, opens the zipper and gets out five, one thousand naira notes and hands them over to Dame): Here have your money.
DAME	*(Collects the notes from her and recounts them)* Thank you and please, come again.
FANCY	*(Hurriedly snapping her bag above her left shoulder while looking around to see if she forgot anything)* You bet I will. I will sure hire you for my wedding makeover *(To Flair who is busy looking her over in admiration)* Flair, let's go.
FLAIR	*(Confused)* Let's go where? I'm not coming over with you to some guy's house not well made up Oh!
FANCY	*(Twirls her eyes around)* In your wildest dreams. Who is taking you along? Please escort me to where I'd pick a drop to my guy's family residence.
FLAIR	*(Smiling as she slowly gets up the seat)* Good, now you are talking. Why would I want to come along with you in the first place? I have to be at home before my parents return from work; abii does it seem to you like I live alone?

FANCY	*(Waves her hand in dismissal of Flair's statements)* Are you escorting me or not?
FLAIR	Why else am I rising from my seated position?
FANCY	*(To Dame)* Alright, bye. I'll be seeing you sometime later *(Walks towards the door of the salon and pushes it open)*
FLAIR	*(To Dame)* Okay Dame, I'll see you later
DAME	Yes. Please, come tomorrow so we can talk about you making me a beaded bag; I am serious about it.
FLAIR	*(Smiling charmingly)* Your wish is my command. I wouldn't mind squeezing out a little cash from the monies you get from your clients *(Makes a quick tongue out movement as she hurries after Fancy and light fades)*

END OF SCENE 5

SCENE 6

It is about 4pm in the afternoon.

In Mama Oluaka's Living Room,

It is an exquisitely furnished living room having an Arabian carpet at the centre of the black and spotted white tiled floor with a round centre table made of glass well positioned on the Arabian carpet. A 36 inches LG television is hanging on the wall of the living room beneath it is a hanger containing a GoTv decoder and an LG DVD player each in a layer of the wall-hanger. Below the hangings on the wall is a settee containing an LG stereo and two medium sized speakers. The living room has three leather couches each three-in-one placed on different ends of the room.

Seated in the living room is Dr. Bent, a tall chocolate coloured, slender man of about thirty years old. He is seated on one of the couches having rounded recommended glasses over his eyes. He has on a yellow T-Shirt with the inscription LET'S BEAT CANCER TOGETHER by London Bridge Hospital. This T-shirt of his is left lying over his smart pair of black jeans. His feet are clad in a newly unwrapped white bathroom slipper his mum had made available for him in view of his return. In his mouth is a toothpick. He looks about the living room taking in the beauty of it while his left hand holds a mobile phone to his left ear.

BENT   Hello love, where are you right now? Since that time? Where you're at is not so far from where I live. Wait, wait, you know what, if I do not see you in the next thirty minutes; I will have to come and fetch you myself. What? Could you please give the driver your mobile? Yes. Hello! *Nwoke m, kee* way? Traffic jam! *Kedu ihe butere ya bu* traffic jam? *Ya buru ma okweghi gi; i mee ka m mara* so I can come and pick her up myself. Can I count on you? Okay. Could you please hand the phone over to my fiancée? Honey, just hold on tight; he's assured me he will get you here in no time. But like I said, if in thirty minutes' time I do not see you; then be rest assured; I will be on my way to you. Alright dear! Till later!

(Mama Oluaka enters the living room wearing a yellow buba gown; a mobile phone in hand. She sits in another cushion opposite her son)

BENT   *(Shaking his legs slowly while looking warmly at his mum):* Mama, you've done noble Oh!

SCENE 6

                       Thanks so much mum for that delicious oha soup you made. I will have it for lunch tomorrow and the day after and the next and the next.

MAMA OLUAKA *(Pleasantly thrilled)* Oh! Yeah!

BENT *(Nodding in approval)* Yeah Mama! *(Looks about the living room in admiration)* Mum, you're a wonder! Look how you've transformed this place. Chai! Mama, *i di* too much! *(Raises his right thumb at her)*

MAMA OLUAKA *(Smiling broadly)* You like what I have done?

BENT *(Nods in agreement)* Nhm! The colours used for the painting are warm, relaxing and very suiting. The arrangements are quite in line. *(Engr. Reward enters the living room looking a bit tired)*

REWARD *(Walks towards Mama Oluaka)* Mum, you're the best of cooks. I enjoyed the oha soup mum, thanks. Please keep some of it refrigerated for me to partake of when next I come.

MAMA OLUAKA *(Looking him up in a knowing way)* And when shall 'when next be?' in a year's time right?

REWARD *(Smiling)* Mum, please don't start. *(Walks to his elder brother and on getting to him, he half bends and extends his hands for a warm hand shake)* Dede, once again you're welcome.

BENT *(Takes his hand in a shake)* Thanks bro. What's popping? You want to check out I perceive.

REWARD *(Shaking his head in acknowledgement)* Big bros. You know now. I got to work. I will be onshore tomorrow and will be off shore in two weeks' time.

BENT I understand. *Nwoke na ife.*

REWARD *i manu Sir. (Straightens up)* So, you will be staying a total of six weeks you said.

BENT *(Nodding)* Very correct.

REWARD *(Smiling)* Good. It means I will still have so much opportunity to be around you then.

BENT Sure!

REWARD Alright Sir. Let me get going. *(Turns from him and begins to walk towards his mother)* Mum, let me get going; it's getting late.

MAMA OLUAKA *(Beginning to miss him)* Won't you hang around some more?

REWARD *(Hesitating)* Mum, don't start again.

MAMA OLUAKA You hardly come around eh, now that I have seen you; you won't stay long enough eh. If you are doing missing in action now that you are still a bachelor, what will happen when you are married eh?

BENT *(Choosing to help out)* Mum, could you please release him. He has to work and provide for you both. I recall when you would always call me and tell me you've been praying for him to get at a lucrative job; now that he's got one; why not let him work and make you

SCENE 6

proud ah, mum?

MAMA OLUAKA *(Shrugs her shoulder in acceptance)* Okay, if you say so.

BENT Yes mum, let him go *(To Reward)* Reward, please get going.

REWARD *(Grateful)* Thanks bro *(Puts his two palms together and raises them up in appreciation)*

BENT *(Makes a movement with his hand)* It's nothing bro. Please be safe!

REWARD *(Nodding and smiling)* Surely! *(To Mama Oluaka)* Mum, let me get going. I'll see you in two weeks' time, okay. *(Goes over to her and gives her a firm hug)*

MAMA OLUAKA *(Patting him on his back)* It's okay son. I understand *(Releasing him from the hug)* You get going okay.

REWARD *(Straightening)* Yeah, right! Okay, the both of you, I am going.

(He heads to the door, opens it and exits)

MAMA OLUAKA *(inquiring)* Nnaa, what are your plans about marriage? You haven't told me anything. Do you not see the need to settle down? Are there no charming, responsible ladies up there?

BENT Mum, I'm on course *(Gets up from the couch and walks to the centre table, gets the remote to the GOTV; walks back to his seat and begins to search for a suitable channel)*: You want to spoil my surprise right?

MAMA OLUAKA *(Taken aback)* Surprise, what are you up to son?
BENT *(Calm as he continues to search for a channel)* Mum, don't you worry yourself; you will get to know by and by.
MAMA OLUAKA What is the surprise about? Anyway, *(Adjusts herself in her seated position)* I wouldn't know if you have found someone and I know I am not in a position to choose a spouse for you; but there's this lady who comes around to buy my bean balls from time to time. She's beautiful, well mannered and hardworking. I think you will like her.
(Dr. Bent is unmoved, his eyes glued to the television set)
MAMA OLUAKA Nnaa, are you with me?
(Dr. Bent Still has his attention to the television)
MAMA OLUAKA *(A little agitated, in a higher pitch)* Nnaa, am I talking to myself?
BENT *(Recovering abruptly as he faces Mama Oluaka)* Mum, Yes, what were you talking about? *(Adjusts his eye glasses)* I am sorry I didn't know you were talking to me, this football match captured my attention.
MAMA OLUAKA *(Gives him a knowing look)* What are your plans regarding marriage?
BENT *(Shaking his head left and right)* My plans regarding marriage... *(His phone rings)* Excuse

SCENE 6

me mum *(He gets up and walks a distance away from his mother and answers the call)* Sweet, where are you? You are where? You know what; you just hold on there; I am on my way. Did you hear me, do not make any further movements; I'm coming to get you, okay.
(He brings down the phone from his left ear and heads back towards his mum) Mum, may I have the car key please?

MAMA OLUAKA *(Surprised)* Car key, are you going out?

BENT *(A little impatient)* Yes mum, I have someone I need to pick up.

MAMA OLUAKA *(With a perplexed look)* Someone, you never told me we'd be expecting someone.

BENT Oh! Come on mum, the car key, please. Trust me.

MAMA OLUAKA *(Pointing to the centre table)* There, on the table.

BENT *(Walks to the centre table; picks up the car key and begins to head towards the door phone in hand)*: Mum, I'll be right back and don't you worry, okay.
(Exits)

MAMA OLUAKA *(To herself)* These boys. If you don't take care they'd make you hypertensive *(Heaves a sigh of relief as she gets up, walks to the couch where Bent had left off the remote control; picks it up and gets back to her seat)* *(More*

of a mumble) I hope she can make it down here at this time of the evening. Let me give her a ring first.
(Searches for a contact on her phone and on finding it; she dials the number and puts her phone to her left ear)
Yes. Hello. Flair, is that you on the line? Oh! It is I Mama Akara. Um, are you free? Can you make it to my house at this time? I know it may not be easy for you; but you see; I would love you to get me a beaded bag. You know we talked about it earlier today and I thought why not now. I need you to come see the pattern I want you to make for me. Don't you worry; I know it will be late; but I will drive you back home afterwards. Feel free to send me your mother's number. I will call her and explain to her okay. Let me text you the address now. Alright! I am expecting you.
(She begins to compose a text on her phone as light fades)

END OF SCENE 6

SCENE 7

It's about 5pm.
In Mama Oluaka's Living Room
(Mama Oluaka paces about her living room looking at the walk clock intermittently).

MAMA OLUAKA *(To herself)* Nwaa amaa nraputa m. *(Picks her phone from the centre table and begins to dial Bent's mobile number)* Bent nna m, kee ebe i no? You just came back and you are already out on the road, eh? Biko mere nu m ebere eh; please come back home, please.
(A knock is heard on the door and Mama Oluaka ends her talks with Bent and hastens towards the parlour door)
Who's there? I'm coming *(She opens the door to find Oluchi)*
OLUCHI *(Tired)* Mummy, good evening
MAMA OLUAKA *(Exhales some air looking a bit disappointed)* Welcome nwa ada, please come inside *(She leaves the door-way making way for Oluchi to come in)*

OLUCHI *(Shutting the door after her as she looks her mother over)* Mum, is all well with you, you look tensed.

MAMA OLUAKA *(Pretending to be alright)* I am alright Darling. You just go inside, freshen up and have something to eat *i nugo*.

OLUCHI *(Looking about the living room as though in search of someone or something):* Mum, did brother Bent not return again today? You said he would return today.

MAMA OLUAKA *(Firm)* Nne, you go inside, freshen up and have something to eat, your brother will be home any moment from now okay.

OLUCHI *(Wide eyed)* Really *(Jumps up with glee)* Yes! Brother promised to get me a new, sophisticated phone, yes!

(Begins to walk out of the living room)
I am sure he complimented my work on your face, right?

MAMA OLUAKA *(Rolls her eyes in exasperation)* Yes Oluchi he did; will you get going?

OLUCHI Yes Ma.
(Noticing for the first time that the electrical bulbs were agog with light)
Whoa! There's light! That's good. Mum, there's this series on Zee World that I am following, King of Hearts, it's a very interesting movie. Mum, would you not like to watch it with

SCENE 7

me?
(Mama Oluaka does not reply her but folds her arms and looks blankly at her)
Alright mum, let me get going
(Exits)

MAMA OLUAKA *(Heaves a sigh of relief)* These children won't kill me. And yes, Flair, I haven't seen her yet.
(A knock is heard at the door and Mama Oluaka goes to get it)
Yes. Who is there?

BENT *(From outside the door)* Mum, it's me

MAMA OLUAKA *(Opens the door in haste)* Welcome dear, you almost got me worried.
(Dr. Bent enters in the company of Fancy who follows closely after him, his left hand holding her right hand as he leads her in. Just as they walk into the living room, the electricity light goes off casting a near dark shadow over the living room. Mama Oluaka is surprised seeing a lady with her son. Dr. Bent and Fancy walk towards the very couch he had sat on earlier and gestures to Fancy to sit on the couch; she sits and he sits after her. Mama Oluaka shuts the door and follows them swiftly reclaiming the couch opposite them.)

BENT *(Clears his throat)* Mum good evening, here is *(Hand motioned towards Fancy)* my fiancée

	Fancy, Fancy Umengwu.
MAMA OLUAKA	*(Surprised in a good way, eyes wide open)* Really, you're welcome my daughter; you're welcome. *(To Oluchi who is inside)* Oluchi, Oluchi come Oh! *(Oluchi emerges from within to the living room.)*
OLUCHI	Yes, mum
MAMA OLUAKA	Please come and put up the rechargeable lantern so we can see one another.
OLUCHI	Yes Ma. *(She goes straight to where the rechargeable lantern had been charging, unplugs it and sets it on the centre table. On turning the lantern on she with the faint light it emits catches a glimpse of her elder brother and exclaims in glee)* Brother *(Runs towards him)*
BENT	*(Gets up and stretches out his arm for an embrace)* Adanne, kee kwanu?
OLUCHI	*(Refraining from the embrace)* A di m nma Sir. Brother, good evening Sir. Welcome Sir. *(Turns to Fancy who is seated stiff on the couch)* Aunty good evening Ma.
FANCY	*(Smiling stiffly)* Good evening dear.
MAMA OLUAKA	*(To Oluchi in a warm tone)* Oya, go and put on the generator, this lantern is not doing me any good as I can barely pick out the face of our visitor here.

SCENE 7

OLUCHI *(To Mama Oluaka)* But mum, brother Reward used up the last fuel we put in the generator last night while watching a football match.
MAMA OLUAKA Okay, go across the street to the filling station and buy fuel for our use Oh!
OLUCHI *(Nodding)* Yes mummy.
MAMA OLUAKA You know where you will find money now, get out a thousand Naira and buy all of it, hurry so you can find time to eat I know you haven't eaten or have you?
OLUCHI *(Shaking her head in the negative)* No Mum, I haven't.
MAMA OLUAKA Oya, get running then so you can first get the fuel and then go ahead and eat Oh! Nwa m
OLUCHI Yes Ma
(She exits)
(She emerges again money in hand and begins to walk towards the exit door)
BENT *(Rising from his seated position)* Mum, let me run that errand alongside Oly while you two *(Points towards Fancy)* get along with each other okay.
MAMA OLUAKA *(Acknowledging)* Okay my dear.
(Dr. Bent advances towards Oluchi and they two exit the living room)
MAMA OLUAKA *(To Fancy)* So, my dear you are welcome, once again.

FANCY   *(A little uptight)* Thank you Ma
MAMA OLUAKA *(Warming up)* So, how are you?
FANCY   I am very fine Ma and you?
MAMA OLUAKA *(Smiling)* I am fine my daughter.
                (There is a brief silence)
MAMA OLUAKA *(Breaking the silence)* So, what is with you and my son?
FANCY   *(Through clenched teeth)*: He is my fiancé
MAMA OLUAKA *(A bit surprised)* Are you serious? You two have been dating?
FANCY   *(Nodding)* Yes Ma
MAMA OLUAKA For how long now?
FANCY   About a year
MAMA OLUAKA *(Surprised)* Oh! Really?
FANCY   *(Nodding)* Yes Ma
MAMA OLUAKA *(Beginning to pick interest)* So, where do you come from?
FANCY   Well I am from Ikeadighi Community in Itio Local Government Area of Ziaba State
MAMA OLUAKA Okay that's good to know. So, you love my son?
FANCY   *(Nodding)* Nhm. I do.
MAMA OLUAKA It's good to know. So, you met him where?
FANCY   In Kante mid August last year
MAMA OLUAKA *(Guessing)*: And you are a doctor?
FANCY   No, an Economist
MAMA OLUAKA *(Peering at her)* Do you work in a bank?
FANCY   *(Shakes her head in the negative)* No, no, I

SCENE 7

do not.

MAMA OLUAKA *(Breathes out loudly out of relief)*: Good. I was beginning to get worried. Having a doctor for a husband as a banker woman can be very, very challenging and demanding. It's good to know you are doing something else other than banking, you need time to attend to family, you know.

FANCY *(A little bit excited)* Yes. However, I am not working anyway. I have yet to get at a job.

MAMA OLUAKA You haven't?

FANCY No. I haven't. I just feel I need to be a-stay-at-home mum, you know. So I can take good care of the home.

MAMA OLUAKA *(Beginning to get worried)* Okay! You went to the university am I right?

FANCY Yes. I've got my Master Degree.

MAMA OLUAKA Okay. And you don't think it's important for you to get at a job?

FANCY Well it's not that. It's just that I really want to keep the home in shape so when my husband comes home it would be all nice, neat and tidy

MAMA OLUAKA *(Gives an understanding nod)* You wouldn't need a house help would you?

FANCY *(Surprised)* Why not, I would, I would. They would make the work a whole lot easier.

MAMA OLUAKA *(Worried)* Is it that you sought jobs and did

	not find any that you have decided to be a stay-at-home-mum?
FANCY	*(Smiling broadly)* Well, that too. I have done some searching but asides from that; I just don't think it's right for me to get something doing.
MAMA OLUAKA	And you think it is okay for you not to work?
FANCY	It isn't like I wouldn't like to work but you see; Bent is okay with my decision not to work
MAMA OLUAKA	*(Taken aback)* Really?

(Dr. Bent and Oluchi enter the living room)

BENT	Mum, we're back

(They head towards the backyard to attend to the generator)

MAMA OLUAKA	You are welcome my children *(Faces Fancy)* Did you say, my son, Bent agrees to your not working?
FANCY	*(Nods confidently)* Nnhm

(A knock is heard at the door and Mama Oluaka goes to get it. She opens the door and sees Flair. Mama Oluaka is excited. She ushers her in and shuts the door after her)

MAMA OLUAKA	So, you were able to locate this place?
FLAIR	Yes Ma.
MAMA OLUAKA	*(Delighted)* I am so happy you came around
FLAIR	Thank you Ma. I am also happy to be here. Thank you for deciding to patronize me

SCENE 7

MAMA OLUAKA Alright, this way *(She leads her to the couch where she had been sitting opposite Fancy)* *(Just then, the bulb lights in the parlour come on. Fancy identifies Mama Oluaka and Flair while Flair identifies Fancy. Mama Oluaka is trying to figure out where she met the face opposite her)*
FLAIR *(With surprise)* Fancy!
FANCY *(With fear and surprise)* Flair!
(Mama Oluaka looks at both of them nearly simultaneously)
MAMA OLUAKA You both know each other?
FLAIR *(A little embarrassed)* Yes Ma. She's my best friend. The one with whom I came to purchase bean balls this morning.
MAMA OLUAKA *(Recollecting)* No wonder. I have been wondering where it was I met this face although it is looking all madeover.
(Flair smiles and nods at the same time)
(Dr. Bent enters the living room)
BENT *(Sits close to Fancy and takes her right hand in his left hand and squeezes gently as he looks at her intently)*: My lollipop, you look ravishing.
FANCY *(Warming up)* Thank you Darling
BENT *(Faces Mama Oluaka)* So, mum, how have you both been faring in your getting to know each other talk nnh?

MAMA OLUAKA *(In between gritted teeth)* Very well.
BENT *(Noticing Flair for the first time)* I see you have company.
MAMA OLUAKA Yes. She is a customer of mine and I want her to help me make a beaded bag of white and blue.
BENT Oh! Really? Then she must be good at what she does. Because I know you mum, you always go for the best of stuff.
MAMA OLUAKA (Smiling): Trust me my son.
(Flair looks about Mama Oluaka's living room; taking in all the beauty it exudes)
BENT In that case, I would love her to make one for my baby girl *(Squeezes Fancy's fingers gently but Fancy taps him mildly with her left hand in order to dissuade him from going ahead with the bargain but Dr. Bent doesn't take notice)*
FLAIR *(Coming to terms with Dr. Bent as she smiles benignly)* Thank you so much Sir for your interest in having one of my beaded bags. So, may I know your specifications; what colour, do you want a combination of colours, what shape, is there any pattern or style of bag you have in mind and for what occasion would you like the bag to be carried.
BENT *(With interest)* You speak intelligently and persuasively.

SCENE 7

	(Fancy nudges him but he is not moved) I think I will have to ask my fiancée here what her specifications are (looking at Fancy to ascertain her response)
FANCY	*(A little embarrassed)* I do not think I... I would want...
BENT	*(Teasing her mildly)* Oh! Come off it. It's nothing. *(To Flair)* So, you'll make her one; her favourite colour is blue. Use what specifications you know would suit best. And yes, how much would that cost?
FLAIR	*(Assertively)* Depends on your specifications Sir. I have bags of five thousand, ten thousand, and fifteen thousand all depending on the customer's specification.
BENT	*(Determinedly)* Okay, I will go for the bag worth fifteen thousand; I hope you will do a perfect work.
FLAIR	*(Smiling confidently as she nods)* You can count on me.
BENT	Alright, when shall the bag be handy?
FLAIR	five days tops, depending on the nature of the specification
BENT	*(Nodding)* Oh! I see. So then I will be expecting you in five day's time right?
FLAIR	*(Smiling the more confidently)* Certainly but you haven't chosen any pattern, shape yet?
BENT	You take up whichever pattern, style you

know will suit my Sweet *(Gives Fancy a smile as he squeezes her palm gently).*

FLAIR *(Smiles and nods in acceptance)* Will do sir.

BENT Okay then, so, five days it will be. And am I supposed to give you an upfront payment?

FLAIR Ideally yes. Because you know I am supposed to purchase materials for the work; but I would rather you pay afterwards; I trust that when you see the quality of work I have produced you would agree it's worth more than the fifteen thousand Naira price placed on it. I will have you pay after the work is concluded for the purpose of trust.

BENT *(Surprised)* Good business strategy you've got there.

FLAIR *(Still smiling)* Thank you.

BENT *(Acknowledging)* You're welcome. *(To Mama Oluaka)* Mum, about the discussion *(He makes eye contact between her and Fancy)*: I hope grand right?

MAMA OLUAKA *(In a not too impressed tone)* My dear, perhaps we will talk about it later.

BENT Haba Mum! It's getting late; I have to drive her back to her friend's house. She's staying over at her friend's and shouldn't come back late you know

MAMA OLUAKA *(Gets up from the couch)* Ladies *(Looks Fancy and Flair in the face respectively)* Could

SCENE 7

you both please have I and my son excused for a moment? We'd be right back, okay.
(Flair nods, Fancy is too perplexed to make any movement)
(To her son) Bent, can I have a word with you

BENT   Sure mum, why not *(Hurriedly gets up the couch)*
(They both walk out of the living room Mama OLUAKA leading the walk followed closely by her son)

FLAIR   *(in a low surprised tone)* What are you doing here Fancy?

FANCY   *(With a bit of loath in her tone)* What I am doing here? I am here with my fiancé; isn't that obvious.

FLAIR   *(heaves a sigh of relief)* Hmm, it's really a small world! So, your guy is my customer's son.

FANCY   *(Embarrassed)* Yeah, the Mama Akara's son. Gosh! *(Fans herself with her left hand)* With all that English! Come to think of it; I thought she was unschooled.

FLAIR   *(Surprised as she keeps looking about the living room in admiration)* Things may not really be as they appear. To think that the woman whose shop you belittled this morning and whose fingers you cursed lives in a place such as this and birthed the man whom you love *(Looks Fancy over with her eyes saying, 'You should have known better not to berate people')*

FANCY *(Beginning to get her vibes on):* And what exactly are you trying to insinuate?

FLAIR *(Feigning innocent)* Nothing Flair. Just that, I mean come to think of it, the woman with the crooked, rocky-like finger is going to be your mum-in-law.

FANCY *(Looks down humiliated)* Why didn't Bent do something about his mother's shop. That place is appalling. I will tell him to do something about it asap.

FLAIR *(Surprised)* I see you really are concerned about the state of her shop and to think that that's coming from someone who doesn't intend to *(She mimics Fancy by tenderly pampering her hands)* soil her hands.

FANCY *(Clearly annoyed)* Stop Flair! This isn't funny.

FLAIR *(Sober)* I am sorry.

(In Mama Oluaka's Corridor, she and her son converse)

BENT *(Anxious)* Mama, what is it?

MAMA OLUAKA Bent, Bent, Bent *nwa m*, you said the lady there is who?

BENT My fiancée

MAMA OLUAKA Really?

SCENE 7

BENT   Yeah!
MAMA OLUAKA   You would rather have a woman who lacks industriousness as wife
BENT   Mum, how do you mean? She's a graduate, a master degree holder at that.
MAMA OLUAKA   And who eats certificate, ehn, Bent *nwa m*?

BENT   She'll find a job
MAMA OLUAKA   *(Stumping her feet; hands akimbo)* Really, you think so? She doesn't speak like one who's interested in doing any work.
BENT   *(Concerned)* Mum, how do you mean?
MAMA OLUAKA   You want to know what I mean. Alright, let's get back inside the living room *(She leads the way as her son follows)*.

(Inside the living room)
(Mama OLUAKA enters the living room followed after by her son. She reclaims the couch she had sat up from while her son takes his position beside his fiancée. He reclaims her left hand and squeezes her fingers mildly in order to give her some form of comfort, reassurance).

FLAIR   *(To Mama OLUAKA)* Ma, may I have your specifications and see what style you would have me make for you so I can get going please? It's getting dark and my parents will begin to get worried for me.

MAMA OLUAKA *(In an assuring voice)* Don't worry my dear, my son will drop you off okay.

FLAIR *(Swallows a gulp of sputum as she nods quietly)* Yes Ma.

MAMA OLUAKA *(To Fancy)* So, my dear, what do you say you do for a living?

FANCY *(Swallows a gulp of saliva)* Ma, I am not working for now.

MAMA OLUAKA And you would like to work, right, you know make a living, earn some money?

FANCY *(Reluctantly as she shifts uneasily in the seat)* Yes!

FLAIR *(To Mama OLUAKA in a low tone)* Ma, can I not wait outside; I believe you are having a private discussion with your family.

MAMA OLUAKA *(Reassuring)* It's nothing my dear. Feel free to be a part of my family for today.

FLAIR *(Swallows and readjusts her sitting position)* Yes Ma.

MAMA OLUAKA *(Facing Flair, face stern)* You are a master degree holder; am I correct?

FANCY *(Holds Dr. Bent's hands tightly for support)* Yes

MAMA OLUAKA When did you obtain this degree?

FANCY last year

MAMA OLUAKA And before you went for your master degree, where you working, did you find something doing?

SCENE 7

FANCY *(Shrugs her shoulders)* No, why?

MAMA OLUAKA Well, I just want to know. I suppose you immediately got at a Master's scholarship immediately after you left school right?

BENT *(Worried)* Mum, I don't get you, why all these questions? What are you trying to prove?

MAMA OLUAKA I am getting to know your fiancée Bent; shouldn't I ask questions to get to know her?

BENT *(Pensive)* Yes mum you should but all these kind of questions about work; I don't get it mum? Is it a must that I'll have to settle down with a working class? She has not been fortunate to get a job for now but when she joins me over there, she sure will get one, okay, so, please let her be.

(Fancy smiles mischievously)

MAMA OLUAKA Bent, would you have me continue to get to know this fiancée of yours or do I leave the two of you to each other?

BENT *(Exasperated)* Mum, it isn't that I do not want the two of you to get along; I mean it's the very reason I requested of her to come over in the first place; but mum take it easy on her.

MAMA OLUAKA *(Readjusting her sitting position)* Look here dear *(To Fancy)* I have nothing against you; I just want to ensure my son is with someone who values industriousness. So, do you work,

	what are your work ethics?
	(Flair heaves a sigh of exasperation)
FANCY	*(Wiping the sweat beads that were beginning to gather in her forehead with her free left hand)* I…I…I work, only I am not working now, maybe sometime in the future
MAMA OLUAKA	Alright my dear, perhaps I should tell you a little story. My son here *(points at Bent)* whom you obviously love is a product of my work; I did hard work; I am sure you know what I do for a living; I sell fries. It was the money I garnered from doing several businesses before I eventually landed me the frying business that I was able to pay my son's fees, buy his textbooks and the likes. I am sure you do not like the idea of me frying stuff, do you? *(Fancy swallows and is silent while Flair looks about the parlour to keep away her interest from the current brouhaha)* I sold bend-down-select-wares from office to office to get at money; at a time I did a nanny job in the morning and roasted corn and pear in the evening. I was a widow having just lost my husband who was the bread winner at the time; it was my hard work that made the doctor you see today and obviously admire. When you get to what you see as my office; it doesn't look like what you

SCENE 7

would admire; but that's the same place from whence I got monies to send to this young man you fell in love with while he was in med school. I have made no face lift; he today can provide me with all the facelifts I need to make that place a relax and eat place but I chose otherwise; and do I make money? If I recall it was my tasty akara that brought you to my shop this morning. So, the question is, should he die tomorrow after having married you and left you with kids; would you still be able to take care of your children, train them up properly or would you quickly bow out to find greener pastures somewhere else, with someone else leaving berserk his children?

(Dr. Bent looks at Fancy still holding her right hand in his left hand).

FANCY *(Swallows again)* I... I...believe that when I get to that bridge that I will cross it.

BENT *(To Fancy in a low appealing tone)* Come on Fancy, say something tangible

FANCY *(To him)* That's the best I can say. They are my kids. Should such a thing happen, I believe I will do what is in their best interest as well as mine.

BENT *(To Fancy, still appealing looking her straight in the eye)* And what could that possibly be?

FANCY	*(Overwhelmed, left hand to head in frustration)* I don't know. I just can't think straight right now. *(In a louder tone)* And why all these questions about work, work, work. How about love, whatever happened to love. Isn't that the reason why we are choosing to get married to each other; it's because we love each other.
MAMA OLUAKA	Marriage is work my dear, love notwithstanding. A wise woman builds her home, building is work.
BENT	*(To Fancy, in a low tone not mindful of his mother's words)* You know what, what if I started up a business for you when we get over there, or probably you choose to learn a skill to keep you busy, I don't know, anything so, you could have something doing while we wait on your getting at a white collar job.
FANCY	But honey, I can't do that. I am not one of those cut out for businesses, okay. I'm an Economist. I will do a desk job.
BENT	*(Nodding in agreement)* Don't you worry, we will find one eventually.
FANCY	*(Smiles hopefully)* Yes, we will.
BENT	*(Facing his mum)* So, we will find a job when we get back.
MAMA OLUAKA	*(Sneering as she looks at them both under her eyes)* And when would that be that she would finally get her papers and join you abroad eh?

SCENE 7

                Say six months, one year? And in those months you would have to fend for her right and then when she gets over there; she would also have to wait for say another six months, one year before she finally gets her hands on a desk job right?

FANCY   *(Over board)* How we live our life, what's that to you Ma'am, huh?

(Flair is wide eyed in disbelief)

MAMA OLUAKA *(Smiling bitterly)* Can you hear her? Can you hear what your Economist fiancée is railing at your mother, you haven't even married her yet eh?

FANCY   *(Slides her right hand off Bent's as she raises both hands in frustration)* I've had enough mama, I've had enough for one evening. All I hear is work this, work that; I'm not cut out for that shit okay.

(Dr. Bent is distraught as he looks as Fancy in bewilderment)

MAMA OLUAKA *(Gets up in anger and begins to walk out of the parlour)* I will not be insulted in my own house.

BENT   *(Rises and follows after his mother)* Mum, don't walk out on us, mum, please.

FLAIR   *(To Fancy)* What do you think you are doing? Have you gone out of your mind? You're supposed to be all loyal and meek. You mustn't

	spill everything out.
FANCY	*(Irritated)* Oh! Please cut me some slack. So this is your plan after all. You and her, you want to go for my Bent right. It ain't gonna happen. You hear me? It ain't gonna happen. So, she was rooting you for him, Oh! My gosh!
	(Flair is flabbergasted and keeps quiet)
	(Inside the Corridor)
	(Dr. Bent walks past his mum and comes face to face with her)
BENT	Mum, this is the woman that I love that you are handling the way you have.
MAMA OLUAKA	My dear, are you sure she loves you? A woman who genuinely loves a man will do all in her power to keep him and based on what I just saw she doesn't quite seem to be that woman.
BENT	*(Trying frankly to exonerate Fancy)* She obviously must have been terrified with all those questions
MAMA OLUAKA	*(Perplexed)* Son, you know I am not an illiterate, don't you? You know that your dad would not have me work even though I wanted to; but then when he died what happened? Did his relatives leave us with anything? By the time of his death I had almost past market job value; but I knew you

SCENE 7

and your younger ones needed to be fed, taken care off. So, I worked. You know of days I had to apply for teaching jobs and did teach for sometime but because the salary was not enough for the upkeep of the home I started to trade. When I saw what profit I made from trading, I chose to forego teaching to trade.

BENT *(Acknowledging)* Look mum I know all these. But please can you...

MAMA OLUAKA *(Interjecting)* I have nothing else to say to both of you. Let me attend to my guest it's getting late. *(Heads back to the parlour while DR. BENT follows suit)*

MAMA OLUAKA *(To Flair)* So, my dear can you stay some more, or would you be going? We could talk about this bag thing later tomorrow.

FLAIR *(Getting off the chair in haste)* Tomorrow, let it be Ma; it is already very late, my parents will be worried

MAMA OLUAKA Of course they will be, please you get going

BENT *(To Flair)* At least can I do you the service of dropping you off. I'm sorry our discussion ate into your time

FLAIR *(Flatly)* No, no, please. I will just hail a shuttle and in no time I will be in my house.

BENT *(Insisting)* Are you sure you wouldn't mind?

(Fancy looks at the duo of Dr. Bent and Flair with suspicion in her eyes)

MAMA OLUAKA   My daughter why not let him drop you, eh, what is there; it will not only save your money but it will save your time.
FLAIR   *(Flatly, yet again)* No. Thank you *(She begins to head towards the door with Mama OLUAKA following directly behind her)*
    (Dr. Bent goes over to the table and picks the car key and begins to walk towards his mother and Flair whose backs are turned to him)
FANCY   *(Getting up in rage)* And just what do you think you are doing Bent?
BENT   I would like to drop her off
FANCY   Why?
BENT   She's stayed long and I need to assist her. It's dark.
FANCY   Who is she to you that you're suddenly worried about her? And me, when do I get to get back to my place?
BENT   *(Heaves a sigh)* We are talking about my mum's customer who is to make a bag for you, Fancy.
FANCY   *(Holding his left hand with both her hands)* Don't go, she can very well take care of herself
BENT   *(Gently takes her hands off him with his free hand)* Don't be weird. *(Begins to follow after the duo of Mama OLUAKA and Flair)*
FANCY   No Bent, don't leave me.
BENT   *(Stops in his tracks annoyed)* Why are you

111

SCENE 7

	acting paranoid?
FANCY	You don't know that lady so why on earth are you choosing to chauffeur her?
BENT	*(Serious)* am I supposed to re-explain that to you?
FANCY	*(Nodding sheepishly)* Nhn.
BENT	Oh! Come on, give me a break *(He turns and continues to walk towards his mum and Flair while Fancy slumps in the living room with a loud thud.)*
BENT	*(Half running back to Fancy)* Fancy, Fancy *(Shaking her)*

(Mama Oluaka and Flair run back to the living room towards Fancy and Bent who has carried her up as he makes to lay her on the couch as Final Light Fades)

END OF SCENE 7

EPILOGUE

(It is evening and a few persons walk past the stage; four of such persons all young men have on their shoulders a coffin; the young men carrying the coffin look forward, face gloomy from grief. Behind the four young men carrying the coffin is the clown dressed in a long flowing blue gown with the inscription "WORK" written all over it. She steps aside, looks about her furtively as though not intending to be found out.)

SLUGGARD   *(To no one in particular)*: This is he *(Pointing towards the coffin)*: Yes, he, you know him full well. It was but a forth night ago I told him to take me that I was gainful; but he would none of me. But today there, *(Still pointing towards the coffin)* there, lying in that coffin is his remains. He took to the bets as he said he would; he learnt the tactics, the rudiments of the game and did win; huge money they said he won; this was but yesterday, yes, yesterday. But today, he is gone, gone to the beyond. If only he had listened to me; if only he had hearkened to

epilogue

me; perhaps, just perhaps he would be living. I told him that the sleep of a labouring man is sleep but he chose the sleep of death. *(Looks about him furtively yet again and continues)* Yes, he won huge money, at the mention of the said amount; he was said to have slumped and died, ah! Yes! You heard me right, he went dead just at the news and today he is buried with such an expensive coffin, yes, very expensive but to what purpose? Whom did his money benefit? Did it benefit him, or his siblings? Based on this I so warn you, yes you, choose labour, choose work, find something meaningful, worthy doing, don't settle for vanities; but choose me. Why would you die?

(She looks about furtively again and being convinced that she had said enough rejoins her walk behind the four young men bearing the coffin on their shoulders as light fades.)

END OF EPILOGUE

GLOSSARY OF TERMS

Mama Akara - A woman who sells bean balls
Jara   - A slang/ coinage meaning addition/ bonus/ extra
Ahiaomana ere onweya - A good product/stuff/ware sells itself
Oly, nwa m, biko – Oly, my child, please
Nwaazuluazu – A well/ properly trained/behaved child
Ahiaoma   – Good market/ good sales/ favourable sales
Oha   – African rosewood leaves
Keekaimee   – How are you? /how are you faring? / How do you do?
A di m nma   – I am fine/ I'm fine
A naeme nu   – Let's keep trying/let's keep going
Jehovah buEze – Jehovah is Lord
O buezie   – It is true
Lee nke a   – Look at this (one)
Oya   – a slang/coinage meaning quick, hasten up
Haba!   – a slang/coinage meaning surprise
Oyibo   – Whiteman/foreigner
Abeg   – a slang/coinage meaning please
Aka ajaajabutereonunmanunmanu – Hardwork brings success/ it is the hand that toils that eats
Onyeori   – thief
Ah! Ah! Keeihenmaanyianaakogheri eh – Ah! Ah! -What is this old woman talking about/ why is this old woman blabbing
inurunanmaduzuruori I naajukeeiheomee? – You heard/

GLOSSARY OF TERMS

learnt (that) someone stole and you ask what he has done.
Ntioshirigi? – Are you deaf/ Are you hard of hearing?
Enwereihenaeme gin a nti? – Is something wrong with your ears? Do you have a hearing defect? / are you hard of hearing?
Biko, onyemalunwanyi a kpopuyaebeakitaatupu m mawaayaanya – Please, anyone who knows this woman should take her out of here least I give her a befitting slap in the eye.
Kpopu – Take...out
Commot – Pidgin English meaning leave
Wan – Pidgin English meaning want to
Nwanyiasiebeapuakitaa – This woman, leave here right now/ at once/ immediately/ this instance
O dikaaranaagbagi – It seems like/it appears that you are going/running mad/ raving mad/mentally ill
A no m ebea, a naagwagihapu ... aka – I was here all the while when you were told to leave ... alone
ikanaezuzughari – You were still misbehaving
Keeifenaemegin'isi – What is wrong with your head? / Have you lost it all together? / What's wrong with you?
inaawiala – Are you going crazy? / are you raving mad? / are you insane?
Ngwa, tutuluefegisiebe a pua – quickly, pick up your clothes and leave here (this place) immediately/at once/ this instance
Umu m – My children
Abii – slang/coinage meaning not so?/ isn't that so? / is that not true?

imanuaga nu epugodiuzogbaayaotokaanyi new ikeikiri, imanu – You know, they would have to first of all strip her naked, so we can take a good glimpse of (at her)… you know what I mean
Taa mashie gionu – Will you keep your mouth shut
OkiiApari - Old, senseless man
Nee odikaokwusigin'onunaaputa–Can you imagine/ Take a good look at the kind of words that are reeling out of your mouth
A ma m naighotaraihe m mee mean – I know you understand what I mean
A naekwuihebarauruinaakoihenaagbakamoto - We are talking about/ discussing something important and you are ranting about something irrelevant
Nnaa... keekwanu – My man, how are you doing/faring?
Onweghi di – All is well/ nothing is the problem
Keemakandia – How are your people?
Ha no ya – They are there/around/fine
Mama enwekwaranukayabuihe di eh? –The situation appears/looks awkward
Kedukanmadugaejigachaamahadum o putabidobughariwa carton gala na park na ere ma o bun a e mixierisimentina building site eh? – How can a graduate of a university on leaving school go about making money by hawking food items such as gala about the car parks or go about serving as labourers in a place where a house building project is ongoing
O kwesiriekwesi? – Is it right/proper?
A sinaonyeoribuonyeori. O so ginye ye ten million, o so

GLOSSARY OF TERMS

ginyeye twenty; o ganaezuori – It is said that a thief will always remain a thief irrespective of how much money he has access to.
O naadinaobara, hoohaa! – It's in the blood, simple!
Enwereonyenaabuenyeyanmanuanun'onu o sienyeyaagbailu? – Is there anyone to whom honey is given who would prefer to eat bitter kola? Is there anyone who would prefer something bitter to something sweet?
inubeghiakukobanyereumunneanyi no obodooyibondiihe ha naarubuibunshi; ilekotandi mere okenye ma obuilekotarandiochaumu ha eh? – Have you not heard stories of our brethren who leave the shores of our country for foreign nations whose job is to serve as night soil men/ disposers of organic waste; who serve as workers in old people's home and or serve as nannies to the white man's children?
A naamagideuwajoorji – I am taking care to make it appear as though all is well
Nwoke m, kee way? – Young man, how are things with you? / How are you faring?
Keduihebutereyabu traffic jam? – What caused/ brought about the traffic jam?
Nwokenaife – A man and his struggles/ responsibilities
Nwaaamaanraputa m – This child will not get (land) me into trouble
Nna m keeebei no? – My father/ dear, where are you?
Biko, mere nu m ebere, ehn – Please, have mercy on me, will you?

Nwaada	– First/ dear daughter
Keekwanu	– How are you?

www.ingramcontent.com/pod-product-compliance
Lightning Source LLC
Chambersburg PA
CBHW071525080526
44588CB00011B/1563